D1625097

DIRECTORS' THEATRE

Books by Judith Cook include

Directors' Theatre
The National Theatre
Women in Shakespeare
Shakespeare's Players
At the Sign of the Swan: An Introduction to
    Shakespeare's Contemporaries
Backstage

JUDITH COOK

DIRECTORS' THEATRE

SIXTEEN LEADING DIRECTORS ON THE
STATE OF
THEATRE IN BRITAIN TODAY

Hodder & Stoughton
LONDON SYDNEY AUCKLAND TORONTO

British Library Cataloguing in Publication Data

Cook, Judith, *1933–*
    Directors' theatre.
    1. Theatre. Directing
    I. Title
    792'.0233

    ISBN 0-340-42383-5
    ISBN 0-340-49232-5 pbk

Published by Hodder and Stoughton,
a division of Hodder and Stoughton Ltd,
Mill Road, Dunton Green, Sevenoaks, Kent TN13 2YW.
Editorial Office: 47 Bedford Square, London WC1B 3DP.

Photoset by Rowland Phototypesetting Ltd,
Bury St Edmunds, Suffolk.

Printed in Great Britain by Biddles Ltd,
Guildford and King's Lynn.

CONTENTS

INTRODUCTION

It was in 1974 that I first put together a book of interviews with directors on directing. The idea had grown out of a series of features on directors which I had written for the then Arts Page of *The Guardian*.

It was a relatively simple task. There were the obvious choices such as Peter Brook, Peter (now Sir Peter) Hall, Trevor Nunn, John Dexter, etc.; there were those the publishers and I thought a good idea; there were two from the regions and one woman, Joan Littlewood.

By today's standards, the climate for the arts was rather good. No British government has ever given the arts adequate support – and I do not just mean financial – but on the whole governments of all complexions felt that the arts were no bad thing and subsidies continued to rise in real terms. Directors griped somewhat about the level of subsidy and even then with reason. Peter Hall was battling to get the new National Theatre project off the ground; Peter Brook had already given up on Britain and taken himself and his work to Paris where he has based himself ever since. But new theatres were still being built and opened and concepts such as sponsorship and enterprise, if considered at all, were thought to apply mainly to professional sport.

Where are they now, those directors from the original book? Peter Hall has just left the National Theatre and is already set on a West End project. Trevor Nunn, having become internationally famous for musicals, which he had not even attempted in 1974, has stood down as artistic director of the Royal Shakespeare Company. John Barton directs little

7

these days. John Dexter, David Jones and Robin Phillips have worked largely abroad, particularly in the United States. Joan Littlewood lives retired in France, following the death of her husband, Gerry Raffles. Patrick Garland and Clifford Williams have continued to work here and abroad and Peter Cheeseman is still in Stoke-on-Trent, although now in a splendid new "Vic". James Cellan Jones stayed with television and Jonathan Miller, while regularly saying he is giving up the theatre to return to medicine, returns as regularly to the theatre and, at the time of writing, is running interesting and successful seasons at the Old Vic.

This book covers different people – with the exception of one – and different ground. It is noticeable that while politics and finance were mentioned only in passing by directors in the first book, a large proportion of the people now interviewed feel impelled by the changed climate to comment on both. They are worried about having to raise so much money themselves and concerned that sponsorship may affect their freedom to put on what they want. They find the narrow-mindedness and intolerance of the age very alarming, not least the implications of Clause 29 and what "promoting homosexuality" actually means in law – putting on Marlowe's *Edward II*? Most of all, they feel the chill wind of an encouraged philistinism sweeping around them, epitomised, as one interviewee points out, by a Cabinet, one of whose past members went on record saying he could see no difference between a page three pin-up and a Titian.

In spite of this cold climate, however, good things are happening. A supposed received truth is that people no longer (and probably never did) care for Shakespeare, other than the few enthusiasts who go to the Royal Shakespeare Theatre in Stratford and schools forced to go to see the set books performed by the local rep (if the local rep can now get the money). Yet two new major touring companies have put the lie to this. First, came the Michael Bogdanov/Michael Pennington English Shakespeare Company which started out from the Theatre Royal in Plymouth in the autumn of 1986 and is still going strong – and performing all Shakespeare's historical plays about English kings except for *King John*. At a recent visit to the Hippodrome in Birmingham, a two-thousand-seat theatre, every seat was sold for a performance of *Richard II*.

Next came the Renaissance Theatre Company, started by the enthusiasm of the gifted young actor, Kenneth Branagh, whose bright idea of getting experienced and highly talented actors to direct Shakespeare themselves after years of being directed by others, resulted in three remarkable productions: Judi Dench's *Much Ado About Nothing*, Derek Jacobi's *Hamlet* and Geraldine McEwan's *As You Like It*. These, too, have played to packed houses.

Very noticeable this time is, at last, the growing number of women directors. It is, I hope, interesting to include three such different women. Wendy Toye has now been working in the theatre for over sixty years, a range of experience rarely paralleled. Judi Dench brought to her first production her own very special experience of playing Shakespeare in general and Beatrice in particular. Deborah Warner, young and up-and-coming, has been widely hailed as one of the finest directors of Shakespeare to be seen working anywhere in this country today.

As to the rest, this time the range is much wider. Only Peter Hall appeared in the first book and is also included here, in part because he has just left the National Theatre. Welcomed to this one is his successor, the gifted Richard Eyre. Michael Bogdanov is a talent who cannot be ignored and he could not be left out. The Royal Shakespeare Company have produced a clutch of bright directors and my choice for this book has been Bill Alexander, John Caird and Adrian Noble along with Howard Davies who, at the time of writing, has recently left the RSC for the National Theatre.

Also directing at the National is Alan Ayckbourn, an example of playwright turned director. To illustrate how the regional theatres continue to feed the nationals, there is Nick Hytner who began with Manchester Royal Exchange and now also directs for the RSC, the English National Opera and the Royal Opera.

Two directors of very dissimilar community repertory theatres are Philip Hedley who assumed, with some reluctance, the mantle of Joan Littlewood at the Theatre Royal Stratford East, and Roger Redfarn who runs the Theatre Royal in Plymouth. Both took on theatres with huge budget deficits and falling audiences. Both have reversed the trends but in totally different ways. Philip Hedley (who is often described as a "missionary") has made no compromises to what he considers to be the Establishment and says of sponsorship, "the only firm that showed interest in our theatre was a firm of solicitors acting for the Police Federation!" He has made his theatre into a true community theatre which serves its local audience first.

The taxi driver who took Roger Redfarn to *his* Theatre Royal on his first day there said, "I shouldn't work there, if I were you. Nobody goes." His policy has been quite different from that of Philip Hedley but his theatre is also now the centre of his community. In both cases these directors, who are responsible for considerably more than directing plays, have a good deal to say about running their theatres.

Last to be mentioned here, but certainly by no means least, is the anarchic Declan Donnellan whose small touring company has now become nationally respected by audiences and critics alike. He, too, tours Shakespeare (among other things) but you would never mistake a Donnellan production for that of anyone else.

Of necessity I had to limit my choice for this book and there are obviously many other directors of equal merit who could have been included. The selection has been my own and I hope it shows that, in spite of all that is happening in this country today, theatre is alive and well and there is absolutely no shortage whatsoever of talent.

PUBLISHERS' NOTE

Judith Cook conducted the interviews for this book during 1988. Directors' forthcoming plans, as discussed by them, may have changed by the time of publication.

References in the text to Clause 28/29 refer to the debate on the Local Government Bill before it became Section 2a of the Local Government Act, 1988.

PETER HALL

Directed over twenty productions while at Cambridge. First professional production at Theatre Royal, Windsor, in 1953. Worked at the Arts Theatre, London, 1954–6, then Shakespeare Memorial Theatre, directing *Cymbeline* (1957), *Twelfth Night* (1958), *A Midsummer Night's Dream*, *Coriolanus* (1959). As Managing Director 1960–8 created the Royal Shakespeare Company to act as a permanent company playing at the Aldwych and Stratford-upon-Avon. His many credits at this time include the remarkable combination of plays which became *The Wars of the Roses* (1964). Opera productions at Covent Garden included *Moses and Aaron* (1965), *The Magic Flute* (1966), *The Knot Garden* (1970), *Tristan and Isolde* (1971). Appointed director of the National Theatre in 1973 where he has directed many outstanding productions. Knighted in 1977. Succeeded at the National in 1987 by Richard Eyre. With Alan Ayckbourn founding new company based on the Haymarket in London in 1989.

———————————◆———————————

The only director to appear in this book who was also in the last, is Peter Hall and for a very definite reason. When he spoke to me for the previous edition he was just about to move into the new National Theatre building on the South Bank. This time as we talked he was giving up his directorship of the National and handing over the torch to Richard Eyre. It seemed apposite, therefore, to look at his achievements as well as his working methods.

13

The entry into the new South Bank building was a stormy one. It was late, funding had been uncertain, reams were written by its critics about what they considered to be the horrors of the building. Even in those days – and they seem positively Illyrian compared to the present – there were plenty of good, honest British philistines ready to beat their chests and shout that it was all a complete waste of money.

Yet, in spite of it all, the National has been a success. Probably no other civilised country in the world would so excoriate the person responsible for that success nor treat him with such petty vindictiveness.

Peter Hall has dominated the world of subsidised theatre since, in 1958, he took over the single Stratford company which was to become the Royal Shakespeare Company. From there he went on to a brief spell at the Royal Opera House before taking over the National from Laurence Olivier fifteen years ago. It is an unmatched record.

He was born in Bury St Edmunds, Suffolk, the son of a railwayman, and he knew what he wanted to do from an early age. "It was a combination of instinct and ignorance equally compounded. I was very stage-struck and liked going to the theatre, was interested in acting, music – especially music – and design but I never wanted to be an actor. I discovered fairly early on that there was someone behind the scenes who was, in some sense, responsible for all that was happening and I was about fourteen when I decided I wanted to be a director. I don't mean that I knew what wanting to be a director *was* at fourteen, but I remember I read quite a lot about Craig when I was fifteen or sixteen. I read all his published work along with another book which came out at the end of the war or a little after, called *The Other Theatre* by Norman Marshall. It was about art theatre in England in the thirties and that absolutely fascinated me. To anyone who is stage-struck, descriptions of past theatre always sound marvellous.

"Then I got into reading Stanislavsky and went to an awful lot of theatre. I saw Peter Brook's first production at Stratford which was marvellous, absolutely shattering. I was also very jealous because he was only twenty or so and I was still at school. I saw all the Gielgud seasons at the Haymarket, the Olivier/Richardson seasons at the New and I grew up in the war years in Cambridge where there was a great deal of theatre because of the wartime conditions, also a good deal of amateur theatre, mainly the Marlowe Society."

He spent his National Service in Germany where "I was very impressed because although they had very little food or money, the theatre, as a subsidised part of the community's life, was still operating. I was near Hanover and the opera company was functioning out of the stables of the old Elector of Hanover's Palace. That was the first time I saw *Tristan*. I think everything conspired to make me try to find out what a director was.

"I had no idea whether I could be a director – I shouldn't think any of us have. How could we? And there's no way of training us to be one either, which is, I think, regrettable. Most of my generation became directors by having sufficient *chutzpah* to say in our early twenties, 'I'm a director'. If we kept saying it with sufficient *chutzpah* we were sometimes believed and then we directed plays. We became directors by directing. I think that's an awful waste of other people's talent – the people who are working with you – and a pretty crucifying experience for yourself."

He was a teacher in the RAF, teaching economics and business management "which is pretty unbelievable in a way but I've always been interested in administration and finance. There is a side of a director which is partly administrative. If a director doesn't choose priorities he never gets a play on. Although some directors might hotly contest the fact that they are partly pragmatists, I think they have to be.

"While you're in a situation where you can say, 'Nobody has said "no" to being in my play', you can, in your mind's eye, cast it with the world. But once you have your actors you have to do your work with them and use what you have. That is, in some sense, management. You can't be creative in the theatre without having a management sense. An actor also has to have a sense of management towards himself – learning how to pace himself.

"So why did I want to be a director? Through academic training I had a very strong leaning towards words – by that, I mean words in plays and books. Equally I was fascinated from my teens on with sociology and the community and economics. The only lectures I always attended were those of F. R. Leavis. I was made into an academic by the scholarship rat race, which I suspect was a little more rigorous than it is now. As far as my college was concerned, I was supposed to be an academic not a theatre person. I thought if I didn't make it in the theatre I could always be a teacher, though I didn't really want to teach.

"I've always had the feeling that the coming together of the audience and performer is one of the few opportunities in our society for a debate in live terms. What's done on the stage affects those who do it. You don't get that in any other media. It is that quality of the theatre which, as well as being partly for enjoyment, is part church and part a political meeting, which fascinated me and that has remained. To me there are few things more marvellous than an audience which is actually being lit by a theatrical experience. It doesn't even have to be a very good piece of theatre, but it's an extraordinary thing to observe and marvellously satisfying to sit among an audience which is applauding because it wants to. It's the same when an audience is made helpless with laughter and the craft of the playwright releases such a feeling of joy and happiness that you can hardly believe it."

Since he described the initial experience of choosing a play to me in *Directors' Theatre* there has been no substantial change. His first reaction, he says, is instinctive – whether or not he wants to do that play at that particular time. "I cannot rationalise that instinct. There are plays that you read that you want to do at a certain moment; plays that you don't want to do at that time; plays you think are worth seeing but that you personally do not want to do. It's an instinctive reaction on the first reading. If you have an instinct that you do want to do it, then it's like an actor wanting to play a part

– you can rationalise why you have that instinctive reaction later. Those rationalisations may or may not be true.

"It's rather like asking a writer why he wrote this rather than that. It's the observers of one's work who trace patterns and obsessions, but I think that if we become aware of them ourselves then we are in danger of becoming self-conscious, trendy and cunning – and no longer instinctive.

"There are two different aspects to a director's work. In a modern play his job is to stimulate modern signals of behaviour, and the reflections of that behaviour, which his contemporary has written. It is difficult, but not all that difficult, because your language is the same and what we mean by our signals (our social manners, inflections, expressions) is always the same. But from age to age people's looks actually change – the way they make up, the way they do their hair – and the language of social communication changes too from decade to decade. If you hear a record of somebody speaking in 1930, the accent has an entirely different quality. It was born of a different society, a different way of life. There are a myriad things that change. So the signals we send to each other about social behaviour change too.

"A director's task is to stimulate those signals and edit them so that the play lives. In a modern play that's fairly straightforward. But in an old play, where the signals are different and are not being made to the society for which the play is being performed, the problems are more complex. For example, you have to know what Shakespeare's signals are, and then think of getting them through to a modern audience. That's why I dislike doing Shakespeare in modern dress because although it can illuminate, it cuts so much off as well. It is a simplistic and crude way of making *some* signals operate.

"To interpret and edit these signals when dealing with a classical text requires an enormous amount of study so that you know the social background. You know the society the play was written for and approximately how the audience would have received it. You know what it was about, how it was dressed, what the words actually meant then, as opposed to what they mean now. Many words have changed their meaning in Shakespeare, for instance. So the element of scholarship is important. You have to speak from a knowledge that you wear lightly."

When I spoke to him as he was preparing to go into the new theatre, he was rehearsing *The Tempest* with John Gielgud as Prospero. This time he had just finished directing the three great late Shakespeare plays, *Cymbeline*, *The Winter's Tale* and, once again, *The Tempest*. They had been designed for the National's studio theatre, the Cottesloe, but such had been the demand that he was in the process of transferring the productions to the Olivier Theatre.

He had spoken then about *The Tempest* and his fascination with emblematic theatre and how it had led him to the meaning of the baroque theatre, baroque opera, the masque and the theatre of Inigo Jones – pondering, in fact, on whether or not we had become puritanical about visual theatre, in the way that it had been felt by some Jacobean writers that when Inigo Jones came into the theatre, the writer was driven out. That production had been richly decorated on a grand scale. The 1988 *Tempest* was spare, acted out on a ring of sand in front of a plain blue backcloth, a very different concept indeed.

One point he made then seemed far more apposite to the new production than to the old – that basically *The Tempest* is a bleak play. He saw Prospero then as a man who could invent an infinite number of magic visions and images in order to control harsh reality, yet stopping at the end and wondering what was the point of it all. "He hadn't changed man's nature one whit by making all those shapes. He hadn't changed anything. I find that a very penetrating analysis of the artist in society. He has to do it but once he's done it, it has to be done all over again. He makes nothing that is final."

The present *Tempest* is so pared down from the previous one that I asked him if this was how he had now come to see it. "No, it was simply that I had come to do the play again. I think the first time I did it – giving all honour and due to the wonder of John Gielgud's genius – although he tried to play the very restless, irascible, guilty man that is Prospero it didn't fit on him, it really didn't. So it never quite worked.

"I think this time I was determined to get that as the mainspring of the play. It's a Faust play, a play about someone who has sold his soul and has to reclaim it – about someone who has been given the opportunity to play God and has actually played him and has to redeem himself and is then forgiven. I think that at the end, when he asks for some heavenly music and is given it, that is as important a manifestation of God as the arrival of Jupiter in *Cymbeline*. You have to remember that, in writing *The Tempest*, Shakespeare was dealing with something which was actually blasphemous, so he had to write it very elliptically. Prospero does ask for forgiveness, he does throw away his staff and he does ask for heavenly music – and he is vouchsafed it. There's no question but that it is a sign from God. Just think what it means when Prospero says:

> . . . graves at my command
> Have wak'd their sleepers, op'd and let them forth
> By my so potent Art.

He is saying that he has actually *resurrected* people from the dead! It's an amazing, a terrifying thing to have done. Do I think Shakespeare was aware of this? Oh, absolutely. There's something very neurotic every time Prospero mentions his 'Art', his magic, there's something very strange going on all the time. It's not just a nice old man who dreams up pretty pictures on an island; it is someone who has actually played God, lived on the border line where 'white' magic becomes 'black'. After all, he sets himself up to punish all his enemies.

"I think I got it clearer this time. I don't want to make extravagant claims for my work – it's for other people to see what it is – but I do know when I actually hit a play. It's an almost physical thing and I think I have achieved it in *The Tempest*. It's been well received but I think the fact that it has reversed the accepted view of the play will take time to sink in. It is now quite clear to me that every second of the text fits with this view of what it is and it seems strange that no one has gone this far with it before, although some scholars have gone part way. It *is* a Faust play! A play about a man who has committed the ultimate sin, in fact he has gone further than Faust for he is a man who has actually played God.''

The nearness of the audience to the actor is one of the bonuses of seeing these plays in the Cottesloe and this was particularly notable with *The Tempest* where the audience itself became caught up in Prospero's enchantment. Will the productions not lose something in their transfer to the larger stage? ''The wonderful thing about the plays in the Cottesloe was that there was a large enough space for the rhetorical aspect to take wing – because I don't like chamber Shakespeare – but it was also intimate enough for the actors to be able to speak very quietly sometimes, so there was an extraordinary dynamic range. That can't be so in the Olivier but there are other compensations and I think *The Winter's Tale* is actually better in the Olivier.''

Even fifteen years ago it was apparent to Peter Hall, among others, that the technique of speaking Shakespeare, especially Shakespearean verse, was becoming more and more difficult to hold on to. This is now a very real problem which is very noticeable indeed with many of the younger Royal Shakespeare Company actors at Stratford. ''They just don't do it any more. It means hard work and application and it also means commitment on the part of the director of the theatre and the leading actors, that that's the way to do it, and clearly they don't any more. It's a view they are entitled to but it's rather like saying, 'Well, we'll sing this Mozart aria but it doesn't really matter where we breathe or phrase it.' It's crazy.

''They are no longer taught how to do it at most drama schools and there's so little Shakespeare done in the regions now, because of the cuts, that actors just don't get the tune, or form, or shape of Shakespeare into their heads subconsciously. Very few actors can actually tell you the technique of speaking Shakespeare but when I came into the theatre most actors, by the time they were thirty, had been around enough Shakespeare for some of it to have got into their heads. You had the Richard Pascos, Ian Richardsons. You didn't have to work very hard with them to get the technique absolutely firm. But now young actors, unless they go to the RSC or the National, are not around any Shakespeare at all."

This has meant an additional phase in rehearsal. He had explained earlier how rehearsals fell into two different periods: the first, very free and open where anything that occurred to anybody could be tried in order to find the life of the play, the richest pattern of signals; the second, during the last ten days or so when the director's function becomes editorial and technical, when the signals are edited and many of them discarded. Now, if it is a Shakespeare play, there is an earlier stage. "I have to begin by teaching them what a text is. I can't start rehearsing the play proper for about a month. It's terrible. It's a dying art, a dying technique. The gang of mine from the sixties – Judi Dench, Michael Bryant, Ian Holm and so on – they all know it and can pass it on, but not the present generation. What's going to happen? I think we are probably going into a new decorated age of Shakespeare where the text is cut – designer Shakespeare – and that this will increase.

"It's Shakespeare for immediate consumption. For Shakespeare really to mean something you have to be able to speak the verse correctly, and if you can't do that then you do other things with it, you use visual emblems. It's also a kind of tourist plastic Shakespeare. Although, having said that, I think there has been a swing back in some quarters in the last two or three years to the idea that the text does actually matter, at least so far as the critics are concerned – although I don't know whether this extends as far as the theatres. What distresses me the most is that in the sixties what was called 'the RSC style' was based absolutely on that and on nothing else, and that's completely gone. The RSC don't do it any more. Not only do they not observe the form, they don't even speak the text accurately.

"I don't want to sound like a pedant because I think that if I had to choose between spending an evening in the theatre where the play was well spoken and dead or ill spoken and alive, I'd probably choose the latter – and leave at the interval – because I can't bear mis-scanned Shakespeare. Yet the choice shouldn't be necessary because you should do both." What he has achieved in these latter three productions is great clarity and a cohesion of style seen all too rarely these days. "They are also very quick, we get through a lot of text – we speak the speech 'trippingly on the tongue'. That's very important in Shakespeare. I cannot bear all the pauses in modern productions. I don't know what they're for."

Looking back at his fifteen years at the National, what does he see as his biggest achievement? "Making the place work. And keeping it full. I think I've made the public want it and like it and we've never had a deficit since we came in here – the only time we might have had one was when our grant was cut and it was a deficit in prospect, so I shut the Cottesloe. We've always had huge business and it's always been a thriving place. That's what I'm proudest of and it has not been as easy as it sounds.

"In this envious, bitter, paranoid country of ours, if you say that you kept the place full they say you've sold out, so I would add the caveat that I've kept the place full and I've still been able to do things like *The Oresteia* of Aeschylus or Marlowe's *Tamburlaine*, things that at first sight were not at all commercial. *Pravda* by Howard Brenton and David Hare was also, on the face of it, quite uncommercial but was extremely successful.

"I'm proudest of our record for new plays – we've done more new plays than we've done anything and a lot of them have been in the main houses. There's a difference between being a very talented writer who is able to get a message across in the Cottesloe or in a fringe theatre and being able to take on the Olivier and make it work."

But, most of all, it is the artistic climate which has changed so much since those days when he was waiting to go into the new National. His was almost a lone voice then complaining

about the low priority given to the arts by successive governments, compared with that in most European countries.
Now, as is self-evident, there is a chorus of concern.

"It worries me desperately. The rules have now changed.
It used to be thought that the soul of the country was nurtured
and made healthy by the education system, the broadcasting
services and by the performing arts. It used to be thought by
both parties that a certain amount of money should be spent
on keeping that soul healthy, that it was a reasonable charge.
Now that has changed. It is no longer a reasonable charge;
you can only nourish your soul if it is cost-effective, if it
makes money. Now I can prove very easily that the subsidised
performing arts make money, but they do it in the way
Westminster Abbey makes money. Westminster Abbey is
not cost-effective but it brings in an awful lot of tourists
who generate money around it and the same is true of the
performing arts.

"This government, very reasonably in the late seventies,
said we should combine sponsorship in the private sector
with state subsidy, but what they did not say was that they
were going to make sure that the private sponsorship was
used to reduce public subsidy. So every performing arts
organisation in the country is working at less than its full
capacity. Everyone is starved of cash, everyone is being less
productive than they could be, everyone spends more time
– and therefore more money – chasing round after sponsors
than on doing a play, so the priorities are all wrong. I can
only hope that in ten years' time this will all be seen as a
passing mistake – the fashion of a monetarist society.

"I think we leave very little for ourselves or the rest of the
world but our heritage, our culture and our language, and
the performing arts are a central part of that. It's terrible that
I sit here, as I do, and say to you that I think the Shakespeare
tradition is very seriously threatened because there isn't
enough of it – there's not enough for actors to develop and
there's not enough for audiences to get to know it. If the
majority of Shakespeare is for tourists from overseas who go
to Stratford at the height of the season, you're not going

to have any remaining Shakespeare tradition within this country."

He leaves for the commercial West End and his enterprise with Alan Ayckbourn at the Haymarket Theatre where the winds might well blow even colder than on the South Bank. "I don't think it will be that much colder than it is here. I've had to keep this place eighty per cent full and I shall have to do the same at the Haymarket with the difference that I shan't be running a repertory there. It will be one play at a time for short runs and if it doesn't make enough money it will stop." Possible future plans for the Haymarket may well include plays by Shaw, Wilde, and Chekov. "One is also always looking for good new plays and a lot of my friends are, I hope, writing plays that will see the light of day there. I want to go on with Shakespeare – I can't envisage a life without doing Shakespeare – although how I'll do that I don't know. What I really need is a Shakespeare studio where I can batter young actors into understanding what it's all about – make them understand what is being said so that even if the construction is difficult the audience will understand it too. But I'm not going to be able to do that at the Haymarket."

Much of the antipathy he has engendered from the government and the more overt attacks from its sycophantic supporters may well have been due to his doughty championship of the subsidised theatre. Will he continue fighting? "I think in some ways my fighting days are done. I would no longer be fighting from the right position. I think anyway that one starts to be taken for granted as the person who always stands up and complains -- in a way it's self-defeating. But certainly I will fight for the RSC, the NT and the opera houses with my dying breath if it's any good."

As *The Guardian*'s Michael Billington wrote in a summing up of Peter Hall's years with the National, "the Visigoths are at the gates (indeed they are inside the citadel) and there is no cast-iron guarantee that that network [i.e. the one which Peter Hall, along with Laurence Olivier and George Devine, helped to set up] will not be dismantled in the future. Hall has now found his successor in Richard Eyre at the National. But who,

I wonder, will take on Hall's role as spokesman for subsidised art and invaluable thorn in the flesh of government?" Who indeed?

When I spoke to Peter Hall last time he said it was difficult to assess what he had done, "but I was talking to William Gaskill the other day and he said, 'Well, we're none of us young any more, but at least *we're still here*'. That's something, I suppose."

Twelve years later – in spite of all the vicissitudes – that still holds good.

RICHARD EYRE

Has worked extensively in films and television as well as theatre. Associate Director Royal Lyceum Theatre, Edinburgh, 1967–70. Artistic Director Nottingham Playhouse, 1973–8. Producer-Director BBC's Play for Today, 1978–80, Assistant Director National Theatre, 1980–6, and appointed as Peter Hall's successor as Artistic Director, 1987. Credits include *Comedians* by Trevor Griffiths, *Hamlet*, *The Beggar's Opera* by John Gay and *The Changeling* by Thomas Middleton and the musicals *Guys and Dolls* and *High Society*. Films include *The Ploughman's Lunch* and, for television, *Tumbledown*. Has won numerous Best Director awards.

———————

Not everybody envies Richard Eyre his newest challenge as Director of the National Theatre. With the current state of arts funding it might well be likened to the labours of Sisyphus but looking outside the narrow area of finance, there is no one better qualified to take on the job.

"I worked first for a photographer then I tried to be an actor. I started directing when I was an actor in a company in Leicester at the Leicester Phoenix in 1965. It was a production of *The Knack* by Ann Jellicoe which I did on a Sunday night with a few of the actors, and Clive Perry, who was running the theatre, took me aside and said in his hesitant and halting way, 'I think you should decide whether you want to be a director or an actor and if you take my advice you won't be an actor!' He was quite right . . . Then he suggested I did

The Knack six months after that as a fully-fledged production in the theatre, and I did.

"John Neville saw that production and asked me to go to Nottingham to do a production for schools there and be director of a tour to West Africa for the British Council, but the Biafran war broke out so we went to South-East Asia instead. Then I started to get directing jobs and finally an Arts Council training bursary, and so went back to work as Clive Perry's assistant and with him to the Lyceum Theatre in Edinburgh, which is a splendid theatre. It's beautiful and, not only that, it was properly funded. They were slightly traumatised as they had had Tom Fleming running it for eighteen months, which was an attempt, from scratch, to form an international company in the Athens of the north. That had come a cropper, so Clive's strategy was to build up a conventional rep with ambitions to a high standard and do the world's major classics, plays which had either never been seen or had only rarely been seen in Edinburgh for quite a time.

"So the idea was to go through the repertoire, go through the card as it were, and I was there for about six years doing six or seven shows a year. I was very fortunate for we were properly funded, we had adequate rehearsal time and a large theatre, so I got through an awful lot of the world's major classics."

This, he thinks, is one of the factors which gives him such a catholic taste in plays. "I did so much of the classical repertoire. It's a matter of some irritation to me that when it was announced I was to take over the National, some critics said it was worrying that I had had so little classical experience. Well, I've done a substantial part of the Shakespearean repertoire, the Jacobean repertoire, Shaw and so on – I've done time in those! It's just that they were done out of London and on the whole were not reviewed by London critics. So they tend not to be recorded in the archives, but in my view it doesn't diminish the quality of the work."

He has taken time to develop his working methods. "I'm something of a late starter, even though I did start directing at a comparatively early age, but I never did any directing when I was at university even though I did go to Cambridge, the crucible of British directors, that forcing ground full of hot manure . . . Trevor Nunn was in his last year when I arrived and was already a remote and distinguished figure in the university circuit.

"I think all directing is a skill which is acquired empirically. I've come more and more to think there is a real skill to it although I spent a long time believing the propaganda – that anyone can turn their hand to it, and oh, you've got leverage because you were at Cambridge, and you've had lucky breaks – a kind of conspiracy of reasons as to why I might be a director rather than anyone else. Now, perhaps because I've more confidence in my own abilities, I do believe there is a real, measurable, *métier* which is directing, as there is with conducting, and one not to be derided but to be taken seriously. You see, I'm slightly thrown by actors who say blithely, 'Oh, I think I'll turn my hand to a bit of directing now.' I mean, I'd never dare say, 'I think I'll turn to a bit of acting now', or 'I'll turn to a bit of designing'; it may be the low esteem in which some or many directors are held by some or many actors.

"So I do think it is a real craft which has to be learned, and how could it be anything else? But we're British and there's no proper training in this country, or at least not as there is in some of the East European countries where there are extraordinary theatre schools in which directing is taken very, very seriously and taught as a course over many years. Here, inevitably, you learn on the job. Because it's pragmatic, unless you have a visible system, a practice, a process which can be codified – which, in my view, can be a bit suspect – it's always hard to talk about the process without sounding somehow evasive.

"I would say the casting is sixty to seventy per cent, not just in type and the suitability of an actor's looks and ability for a particular role, but also that you feel you will have a relationship with the actors and that they will fit into some kind of social group. Part of the business of directing is to engage a group of people and engender a happy and homogeneous entity. You have to weld together people with shared aims, so that's the first thing.

"I would say I worked idiosyncratically – I expect most directors do – in that I don't apply any system of work across the board. For me, each play generates its own working process and I'd go about it in a different way. I would generally start off by talking about the play with the cast and with everybody involved, sometimes in great detail, sometimes not. I'm wary in principle of productions that you might label as 'thesis productions', where you set out with an idea, a thesis, and in fact the production is there to demonstrate the validity of the thesis.

"What interests me more is the context of a play, the resonance of the narrative. Take *Hamlet*. Everybody's *Hamlet* is going to be different and it's a play that can be done in a vast number of ways. The story allows me to choose this narrative so, in this case, I would say this is what the story seems to be. You then substantiate it. In the case of the *Hamlet* which I did at the Royal Court some years ago, we dispensed with the ghost. I was obviously obliged to explain that to the cast. I wanted to explain that it wasn't a gratuitous or sensational notion; it was actually drawn from studying the play and considering options in presenting the ghost. It seemed to me that it made considerable sense to a contemporary audience and its relation to the supernatural and also in relation to Hamlet, *vis-à-vis* his own madness. If he were possessed in this way, then there would be every reason for him to doubt his own sanity.

"This sets Hamlet on a knife-edge and the threat of losing control is always there for him. So whether it is *Hamlet* or anything else, I start off by just talking generally. This might actually mean working off the text with acting exercises which relate to it in some way, or it might mean simply sitting around a table mining the text, going over and over it until we were all sure we knew the literal meaning of it. In a classical play it's absolutely essential to understand the literal meaning before you begin to stand on your feet and translate literal meaning into performances with their range of nuances and colour."

How about a totally different kind of text, like Trevor Griffiths' *Comedians*? "We talked to a lot of stand-up comics, we went to clubs . . . but I'm not sure, apart from corroborative evidence, that it was particularly useful in that case, except that it made us feel Trevor's fiction had some kind of basis in real life. You believed, yes, this could have happened. But the actual source of all those characters was just simply out of Manchester working-class life. In respect of mining the characters, there wasn't anything terribly useful in keep watching stand-up comics in miners' welfare clubs, which is where we went. We talked a lot about stand-up comedy and watched a lot of it, but in the end the genesis of that production was a great deal of very, very detailed moment-for-moment work which involved a gradual accumulation of detail of movement and behaviour so that, in the end, it became choreographically a whole. There are extremely demanding formal problems in the first act of that play: never less than seven people are on stage, with the focus being thrown from character to character the whole time.

"As a director, apart from making sure that every second, every atom of behaviour and thought in that room was real, meant something and related between the characters, there was the practical problem of just making sure the audience looked in the right place at the right time. It meant somehow generating the right choreography so that, to some extent, it was directed to ensure that someone was in a particular place, but it was done covertly so that, in the main, it generated itself. So that's one method working.

"Another way is when an idea of the production is engendered by a strong visual image or the image of an action, when the locus of an idea, engendered through the text, gives rise to a very powerful, vital image which is the overriding metaphor for the production. This happened during Middleton's *The Changeling*. The theme of the play is of a world which is underwritten by madness and deprivation of sanity and this has turned into a visual image both literally and metaphorically so that the action of it actually takes place framed by the cells of a madhouse.

"In fact, to go back again to *Hamlet*, when I was working on it I was haunted by the image of Nixon's Inauguration Speech in 1974 when he knew that already the Watergate scandal was bubbling away underneath ready to come to the boil, so my production actually opened with Claudius speaking and directly addressing the audience. That is the kind of analogy which comes from life rather than from art.

"Then another play I did here [at the National] was Dusty Hughes' *The Futurists*, about Russian poets after the Revolution. I started that off with a company of about twenty and allocated to each person an aspect of the play to research. So they went away for a week, each with his or her area of research concerning either the character or the artistic scene of the period, or the work of the CHEKA (the secret police) or the social or political conditions. At the end of the week they all presented their research. It was an invaluable way of gathering information: rather than having me or the author stand up for three hours and tell them it was like this, it meant everybody owned a bit of the play. Also it's very frightening to be asked to give such an account however articulate you are, however confident, to sit at a table in front of twenty other people and say, 'This is the research I've been doing.' Actors on the whole are much better at saying other people's lines.

"That was a terribly useful icebreaker for a company who, on the whole, knew each other but hadn't worked together as a company. It was a kind of trial by fire and a useful way of injecting information into the group.

"Rather than having it pushed at them, they actually shared the information and it was also an invaluable way of getting a huge kaleidoscopic view of the period with a lot of people developing a real passion for, and interest in, the material. They wouldn't have had that had we gone about the rehearsals in a conventional way, with a hierarchical structure where the people with the biggest parts knew most and those with the smallest knew least. This is often the case in a production and there's a danger then that the people on the periphery are entirely alienated.

"All I'm saying really is that every play has its different parameters and criteria, so that you apply different working systems which are infinitely variable."

Has he, then, a particular liking for any period or type of play which has a special appeal? "Well, I adore Chekov's plays. I adore *The Cherry Orchard* in particular. That play seems to me to be the greatest play of the twentieth century because it is about the time on the brink of the new century when absolutely convulsive changes are obviously rumbling in Russian society. It is also about the changes in a predominantly agricultural world and one in which the classes were clearly perceptible and prescribed and legislated for and the transition to one in which there were quite different co-ordinates.

"What the play manages to do is to present twelve characters and actually every single social bracket is represented, from the aristocracy to the lowest peasant. In anyone else's hands, it would be one of the most absurdly schematic of plays, with a representative of every class stratum shoved together in a story about selling off an orchard! It's a symphonic *tour de force* because it takes its theme, develops and transmutes it and passes it from character to character, and develops it through the play in the most extraordinary, fascinating and prescient way, and so makes you feel for the humanity in every character while at the same time taking a rather clear-headed social and political view of it.

"I suppose that play exemplifies the kind of writing that does attract me."

So how free will he be to choose the National's repertoire? "I'll be quite free, not entirely autonomously because I'll be working with David Aukin, who is the executive director, and we'll always have a group of people with whom we will talk about the repertoire. At the moment, it's Peter Gill, Bill Bryden and John Gunter (head of design), Nicholas Wright, who is responsible for new writing, Tony Harrison, to advise on translation and who will be a kind of poet-in-residence, and Howard Davies, from the RSC, so we sit down together. I initiate the ideas and say which plays I have in mind, and there may well be very, very ferocious debate about them but in the end the final choice is mine."

But even getting the repertoire on in the present climate is so difficult. How does he feel? "It is very daunting. But it doesn't really pay to think of it that way round. You've just got to think of the shows you'd like to do and then, if that's the policy, think how it's to be funded, rather than thinking that we've diminishing funds so our ambition must diminish.

"The most depressing part is feeling that you're there on sufferance, that 'we don't really need you'. I remember Harold Wilson had some terrible phrase about the BBC, like, 'we'll have to shorten their leash'. I wouldn't even address that particularly at this government. It's characteristic of the British. It is a very, very odd paradox that this country, which has such a rich theatrical culture, so splendid a literary heritage, unparalleled riches, has, at the same time, the most extraordinary indifference to that culture. I sometimes think that perhaps that's the essence of it. It may be the equivalent of a kind of Eastern European repression which engenders creativity; perhaps in Britain it's a kind of tacit indifference which brings about the same thing. I just don't know.

"It's depressing to know that if we were adequately funded, not have to think, 'Where does the money come from next year?' it could all be so much better. It would also push down seat prices if people really understood that subsidised theatre meant cheap seat prices, irrespective of whether some people can afford to pay fifteen pounds for a seat. Seven pounds fifty across the board would be a proper use of extra subsidy. But it would be just wonderful to know that you weren't on trial and also that the equation wasn't made that public money equals self-indulgence."

ADRIAN NOBLE

Read Drama at Bristol University, trained at the Drama Centre. Worked for two years in Birmingham Community Theatre and then went on the IBA Trainee Director Scheme. Went to Bristol Old Vic where he became an Associate Director. He joined the Royal Shakespeare Company in 1979 as Assistant Director on *As You Like It*, *Romeo and Juliet* and *Hamlet*. In 1980 went to the Royal Exchange in Manchester where he directed Helen Mirren in *The Duchess of Malfi* by John Webster and also directed the same play in Paris. In 1981 directed *Dr Faustus* by Christopher Marlowe in Manchester with Ben Kingsley. During that year he returned to Stratford to direct his first RSC production, Alexander Ostrovsky's *The Forest*. His credits include *A Doll's House* by Henrik Ibsen, *King Lear*, *Macbeth*, *Mephisto* based on the novel by Klaus Mann and the musical *Kiss Me Kate*.

———————————

When I spoke to Adrian Noble, he had just taken up his post as overall director of the Stratford end of the RSC for 1988–9. As well as being in charge of the whole Stratford company, he was also re-directing his production of *Macbeth* and a new version of the *Henry VI–Richard III* history cycle.

After reading drama at Bristol University, he went on to the Drama Centre in London. "I wanted to direct but I didn't know how to set about it. One saw extraordinary theatrical events in which one felt the powers of the actor in operation, and when I saw something like the Brook *A Midsummer*

Night's Dream I realised that I had no idea how to release that creative energy. So I went to the Drama Centre to learn techniques and skills. It's a very good school because it's European based; for instance, you do a lot of Brecht. It's the natural successor to the Old Vic system – those people like Michel Saint-Denis and George Devine.

"We had to do an enormous amount of acting ourselves and a whole series of very demanding tasks, like writing films, designing sets. We had to write and adapt plays. It was very practical but also, curiously, it is the most academic drama school. There's a very serious system of analysis, a set of lectures covering two or three years, which starts with Greek drama and ends up with twentieth-century absurdity. Our first year was spent working entirely on Greek myths, which was particularly marvellous for those who had never been to university and it opened their minds. They started asking, 'Who is Hercules?', 'Who is Zeus?' and suddenly they realised they weren't just old bores from the past but real character types, archetypes of the way we now see character. It was run by people who were truly inspired.

"But the one thing they didn't tell you was how to get a job. I directed a one-act Brecht play and all kinds of directors came and saw it, people from Glasgow, Watford, etc., and they said, 'Give me a ring as soon as you leave and come and have a chat'. I did ring and I did have the chat and, do you know, *I never heard another word!*

"Possibly it was because of the way the Drama Centre worked. They said, 'We won't train you for the theatre as it is but for the theatre as it ought to be' and nobody else attempted anything like that. They believed that theatre should be at the centre of society, that it has a sacred history, that it has a function which relates as much to the spirit of the nation as it does to the politics and entertainment of the nation.

"I believe that totally. I've always believed that.

"On the other hand, there were gaps, things they didn't teach us. They taught us nothing about form, especially verse, things I've since come to know and cherish.

"Anyway, I couldn't get any work in the theatre proper so I spent a couple of years working in community theatre in Birmingham and I just about ran myself into the ground, I actually made myself ill. Then I heard about Thames Television bursaries for directors – it shows how ignorant I was; by that time I was twenty-five yet had never heard of them. I wrote off and they told me about all the grand people who had been given one and I thought, 'That counts me out', but I got one. I've really been fantastically fortunate and worked with so many wonderful people.

"For instance, when I took up the bursary and went to the Bristol Old Vic I worked with Richard Cotterell who is one of the great unsung heroes of the British theatre – the number of people he's given breaks to, like myself, Bob Crowley, Ian Charleston, Zoë Wanamaker – yet the average theatregoer doesn't know about him. He's a great see-er of talent. I went there at the same time as Bob Crowley [the designer] and we teamed up immediately and Richard just gave us the most fantastic shows to do.

"We did *Titus Andronicus*, *A View from the Bridge* then *Timon of Athens*, *The Recruiting Officer*, *The Changeling*, *Comedians*, *Love for Love* . . . He gave us an absolute treasure chest of British theatre and we just did it. It was wonderful. Then I came to a crunch time. Richard and I had great ideas for the Bristol Old Vic but came right up against their board and they just weren't interested. They wanted to know why we didn't do 'West End' plays and we decided that if that was what they wanted they'd better get other people, so we both left.

"So I had nowhere to go. I'd always wanted to come here, to the RSC. I used to hitch-hike up here and sleep outside and queue up to stand at the back. Even now I think of it every time I pass a certain farm near Ettington; once some friends and I just went up and knocked on the door – the nerve of it – and asked if there was somewhere we could spend the night and the farmer let us use his barn. I've kept meaning to thank him. Anyway, I asked the RSC if I could come and they said I'd have to come as an assistant director, so I did. I worked on three productions but then I had another piece of good fortune and met Michael Elliot who asked me to go to Manchester to the Royal Exchange."

Adrian Noble's work in Manchester soon became legendary with a stunning production of Webster's *The Duchess of Malfi*, starring Helen Mirren (which subsequently went to the Roundhouse in London) and, in 1981, a production of Marlowe's *Dr Faustus* with Ben Kingsley. Also in 1981 he directed an amusing play by Ostrovsky, *The Forest*, for the RSC in The Other Place, with Alan Howard, Richard Pasco and Barbara Leigh-Hunt. It went on to the Aldwych and brought him a major award, the first of a number he was to collect.

How does he set about working on a play? "I tend to give the actors quite a strong conceptual line on a play because I feel people respond better to a firm framework. I also think that it's my job: there is a proper interpretative role for the director. I don't believe that the words 'directors' theatre' are dirty words at all, although I think we have brought some of the censure on ourselves. It's rather like drugs: some have nasty side-effects. It happens when a director has achieved power and status which have nothing to do with his job and he has enormous control over money and management and employment of people. Therefore bad directors can get away with all kinds of things and quite natural impulses in actors to act are crushed. That is a very serious problem.

"So I think my job is to work very hard beforehand on the text, and then with the designer, and then with the leading actors, involving them very definitely with the thinking behind the production and the very, very strong idea of it that I have. Once they have grasped the idea they have tremendous freedom within it. I'm a great believer in the inspiration of actors. I actually do believe in acting as an 'inspired' art, about both being inspired and about possession – great acting is about something taking over oneself.

"If too much is forced on to an actor, he just becomes part of a maquette or a glorified video in the director's mind. I think it's different with film, but in the theatre we have to be inspirers of others. You mustn't destroy the basic idea that you have about the play, but the actors have to possess it."

To this end he has attempted a major re-organisation of the way the Stratford company works. The acting company has been divided up into two groups whose "coherence" relates to the group of plays in which the actors will perform and the projects they do. One group is dealing with revolutions in two countries – England during the Wars of the Roses and a modern play about Nicaragua – while the other group will be mainly involved in a series of Restoration plays in the Swan.

"This is partly to try to ensure longer rehearsal periods, but I've also set up training programmes for the younger actors. We're doing a lot of work on verse this year: John Barton's held a whole series of workshops for the company, Cicely Berry's done two, I've taken a sonnet class, so they're getting a constant series of verse workshops, four or five times a week during lunchtimes, where they can learn something of Shakespeare's verse. The work on the sonnets lets them work on the verse without having to worry about characterisation."

The new system is also aimed at strengthening the company for the *Henry VI* and *Richard III* productions which, as *The Plantagenets*, make up Noble's own version of the Wars of the Roses. This is not, he stresses, the same adaptation as used by Peter Hall and John Barton who reduced the three plays to two because, says Noble, they believed that history is a machine which cycles and re-cycles, so they cut out vast amounts of contradictory material in their portrait of rising and falling dynasties. We spoke before *The Plantagenets* went into rehearsal.

"I'm doing my version in collaboration with Charles Wood. I wanted to get a writer involved as I discovered, very early on, that you can't do a linear cut on these plays because you're talking about a large reduction. There are four plays, two of which are longer than *King Lear* . . . Even the shortest of them is three and three-quarters hours long and to try to get them down to three evenings, even with huge cuts, is very difficult indeed. I think that Part I will take us up to the murder of Gloucester, Part 2 virtually to the start of *Richard III* – though we might split it with the death of Henry VI ending Part 2, which would mean that what happened after that would go into Part 3. People would be shocked, I suppose, that *Richard* didn't open with 'Now is the winter of our discontent' . . ."

How does he feel the history cycle will fare when Michael Bogdanov's English Shakespeare Company is also touring them? "Well, that's hard to answer. Shakespeare only wrote thirty-seven plays and the idea of not doing any of the history plays for several years because another company was doing them would be ludicrous. We wouldn't have anything left."

But like Bogdanov, Adrian Noble too sees analogies to today in the plays and is on record explaining what they are. He sees a shape within them which deals with revolution and counter-revolution, the collapse of an empire and the decay of a civilisation at home, the disgrace of one generation and the corruption of the younger and, finally, the handing over to children who become the butchers of the earth. In what happens to Edward IV, the Duke of Clarence and Richard III, he sees the natural inheritance of the children of York. He had already been working on the project for over a year. "Ours will be quite different from the other company's. I think they have done straight cuts and this won't be like that at all."

He is also re-working his *Macbeth*, one of the jewels of the 1987 Stratford season, but this time without Jonathan Pryce. Here too he has worked hard on the verse. "We have tried to get an evaluation of how the form of the verse can help the sense and meaning of the play. I do believe as a matter of principle that writing a play in verse is not just a particular way of organising the page. I believe the very meaning of the play lies within it. Otherwise it's like saying, 'Oh, well, a concerto is just like a symphony where one instrument plays louder than the others'; it's as silly as that. The very form contains the meaning and it has to be appreciated, right down to why that line ends with that word. You don't have actually to do it, end stop it or flow it over, but you have to know it.

Then you can ignore it if you like, but if you do that entirely then you do it at your peril.

"So this year, at least, if a director says to an actor, 'That line ends there and not where you're ending it', I hope he or she will know what that director means." As to mounting a production of *Macbeth* again, he says he has not found it difficult. "No, in a way it's been better. I've loved working on it on both occasions although it's not been as intensive this time. Last time I went in at ten in the morning and we worked until ten at night and we all ate together and that kind of thing, but this has been a very good exploration and they've really responded."

He had not found himself haunted by the superstitions which are supposed to haunt productions of the play. "I think you have to look at certain things but I love tragedies, I suppose because they offer such an absurd view of the world, such an extreme view." As to the occult side of the play, "I don't believe in tabloid theatre, by which I mean you bring it down to a level where people say, 'Oh, it's a bit like this or that'. I think you have to make it fresh somehow so that people feel they've seen it for the first time. And they also have to recognise it as an archetype because I think, in this play, there lies very close under the surface a very strong influence of north-western Christian life. So we created our own occult and rituals, very much as Shakespeare did, and I've based them on quite ordinary, everyday things but also on how they relate to the Christian faith because I think the play is about those principles of magic which lie underneath it.

"It's about transubstantiation, sympathetic magic, visions of the cross, all of which are the basis of Christianity, particularly Roman Catholicism. Shakespeare is such a riddle, you see. He's such a conservative man but he contains within his plays such extraordinary, radical, violent elements, all the more remarkable because they come from a man who was a property owner – you feel he might have been a Tory MP – yet the witches in this play contain such an element for change.

"I told the women who were playing the witches to bring in pictures from newspapers, magazines, and so on of women who were outcast, women in distress, and nine times out of ten somewhere near the women in distress were male soldiers. I didn't give them any idea of what to bring, just images of women on the fringes, women who had been rejected, and mostly the images they brought were those of women in extreme grief, very often with soldiers in the background. It was fascinating for that's the beginning of the play, isn't it? There has been a battle, there are soldiers and there are women who have no place in that world and no reason to respect the judgement, order and hierarchy of that man's world. And it's still there – it's in Beirut, Belfast and Nicaragua. Within that dynamic lies the explosion which is the play."

So why was he about to embark on a Restoration season at the Swan? "Quite simply because it's a response to the world I'm living in. I had the idea almost immediately after the General Election. That sense of '*We're back!!!* We're in for *five more years* . . .' And I thought, that is the spirit of the age that we live in and we've got to recognise it. It seemed to me that that is exactly what it must have been like when the Royalists came back from France and Spain after the Civil War and then they went mad – drinking, fornicating, cheating, lying . . . Beauty? Fuck it! Decency? Fuck it! The older generation? Sod them! Younger brothers hating the older ones because they have more money, the older ones waiting for their fathers to die. Absolutely everything was for sale – and that's the world we live in now. It's all there in those plays so I thought, right, let's go for it."

JOHN CAIRD

Born in Canada and worked in touring, fringe and community theatre there. Trained as an actor at the Bristol Old Vic School but changed to directing. Joined the Royal Shakespeare Company in 1977 working mainly at the Warehouse in London. Worked with Trevor Nunn on two Shakespeare productions in 1977 and 1978 and then in close collaboration with him on *Nicholas Nickleby* which won sixteen awards in the UK and USA, including four Best Director awards for him and Trevor Nunn. Work outside the RSC includes Andrew Lloyd Webber's *Song and Dance*. Recent work includes *The Merchant of Venice* at Stratford, the musical *Les Misérables* (with Trevor Nunn), *Every Man in His Humour* by Ben Jonson in the new Swan Theatre at Stratford.

During an intensive rehearsal period for Ben Jonson's *The New Inn*, actors were to be seen around Stratford deep in research. It is John Caird's way of approaching a play of this kind.

"If the play I am directing is set in a period which is unknown to most of the actors, such as Elizabethan England, or, in the case of *Les Misérables*, early nineteenth-century France, or turn-of-the-century Russia, as in Chekhov, the actors will also be unaware of the social and political conditions which were familiar to their characters. They tend to think as twentieth-century characters would think, making conventional assumptions about 'the old days', and basing their behaviour on only a generalised knowledge of the period.

"So what I sometimes do in these circumstances – and by no means all period plays respond well to this treatment – is to ask each actor to choose and research a subject which is in some way connected with the character he or she is playing. The actors then have to address their assembled colleagues on their chosen topic for ten minutes or so. In this way the whole company becomes expert about the period, and each individual actor becomes expert about the social, political and philosophical background from which their character was originally drawn. The purpose of this method is to inspire actors to base their choices in rehearsal on real knowledge of how their characters may have lived and thought. If actors are sufficiently steeped in the life and times of the period, then they will start instinctively reacting as people then would have done. As a director one isn't constantly having to say, 'No, no, that's wrong!' The responsibility for explanation and teaching is shared by all.

"It also gives the company a collective responsibility for the play and inevitably a real sympathy with the writer's view starts to build up. This can only happen when actors know that what they're doing is real and right, regardless of how the production is eventually costumed or staged. It goes much deeper than what people wear or eat. It's about what they think and believe, what the spiritual and emotional influences are behind the dialogue that they have been given by the playwright. Of course, research is difficult for some actors, but you rarely get serious complaints. Some get very nervous at the report stage! For most actors, performing is one thing, but public-speaking is something else altogether. Others reveal great depths of academic prowess or political acumen. In the end, a company finds out as much about itself as about the topics under discussion.

"To begin with I draw up a list of projects I think would be useful for them to do: the religious disputes of the time, the state of the nation in terms of its foreign policy, scientific discoveries, the accepted astronomical beliefs, the state of the medical profession, what did ordinary people eat and drink (in the case of Elizabethan and Jacobean England, why did they drink so much, and to what extent was alcohol a social anaesthetic?), what were the religious beliefs of the time, what were the philosophical notions, and how did everyone fit in the political and social beehive of the nation? Having chosen their subjects, a collegiate atmosphere begins to develop amongst the actors. They begin to swap research and books.

"Within a few days, the value of all this starts to become clear, as the actors discover things which will make a huge difference to their performance on stage. I love getting this kind of feedback. I would find rehearsals stultifying if the actors just stood around waiting to be told what to do. By appealing to actors' curiosity as well as to their skill, characters can develop much more easily. This kind of research is really just one of the starting points for a whole attitude towards rehearsing which will eventually help to build an arbitrary group of actors into something much more important – a company."

One of the reviews of his production of Ben Jonson's *Every Man in His Humour*, put on by the Royal Shakespeare Company at the Swan in 1986, said that it gave you the feeling of walking down Ludgate Hill, opening a pub door and there you were in Elizabethan England. "I think that is what the actors had begun to feel themselves. Research liberates the actors from pseudo-historical behaviour. They start to behave as ordinary people today would behave, but with all the added background knowledge and details of the period.

"I love Jonson, I always have. I suppose, really, you could say I'm besotted with him. I get such a strong feeling of the man while I'm working on his plays. I almost get the feeling that he moves in during rehearsals. There he is, this spiky colossus, a highly intelligent, vain, but approachable man, who begins to haunt the rehearsal room, as he must actually have done for the original productions of his work. Shakespeare would have been undogmatic about himself and his work and very difficult to tie down. Jonson would have bored your ears off on those subjects. Because he's so candid about his own imagination and his own talent, you don't need to be in touch with the spirit world to know what he wants. The message is so direct. The actors feel that too."

As well as the splendid Jonson plays, John Caird is well known for his collaborations with Trevor Nunn on very large shows, such as the David Edgar adaptation of Charles Dickens' *Nicholas Nickleby* and the musical, *Les Misérables*. How easy, or difficult, is it to work in tandem with another director? How is the work divided?

"When Trevor and I do work together – which actually isn't all that often, we've only done four shows – we often work in tandem in the rehearsal room on the same scene at the same time, but in the case of *Nickleby* it was so enormous that we had to work on separate scenes on our own. Then one of us having kicked off a scene, three weeks later when it was time to rehearse that particular scene again, the other one would do it. In the end, it wasn't possible to tell who had done what or who had had the original idea and developed it to the point that the other one could take over and develop it further, and that was always the real purpose of working together! It will be so when we work together again. We hope to do so, but it would need to be something that needs two directors, not something done for the sake of having us both there.

"It would have to be a project requiring complexity in adaptation, or a very large cast, or a very long script, or perhaps all three. You could hardly do Ibsen's *Hedda Gabler*, for instance, with two directors, and there are many plays where it would be very wrong to have two directors, plays which need an individual directorial vision or a relationship between a director and a particular actor playing a specific part, like Hamlet, for example."

Does he prefer to direct plays outside the modern period or is it just the way it has worked out? "I've done a fair number of modern plays. I've worked on plays by Jonathan Gems, Peter Flannery, Mary O'Malley, John Berger and Nella Bielski, Charles Wood – a fair sprinkling. I enjoyed working with John and Nella on *A Question of Geography* at The Other Place. They came over from France during the rehearsal period and they both had very strong ideas about what the spiritual centre of their work is. But they're also new to the playwrighting trade and are both pretty green when it comes to theatrical practice.

"So they had a useful mixture when they came to rehearsals. They were often certain when they saw a particular scene that it was or was not what they were after. But they were also full of wonder and child-like amazement if what they had originally written became powerfully manifest for them."

I spoke to him just before he left for America to start rehearsing a new *Les Misérables* company, the second all-American company. Did he give American actors the same kind of research projects that he gives to English ones and are there any special difficulties?

"I don't think there is a difference in nationality. I think there is a difference in working with people whose primary experience has been in musicals rather than in legitimate theatre. There are different requirements, in terms of training and company awareness, as to what acting is about."

How do you get round that? "Well, it's horses for courses, really. Most people with wonderful singing voices – which is what we need for *Les Misérables* – will have depended on them as the major staff of life in their careers. Therefore, veracity in acting is not particularly their strong suit. It may be, but it isn't necessarily so. In the end, if an actor has the perfect singing voice for the part, you will be on much stronger ground in teaching that person the rudiments of acting than you will be if you have someone who can act but obviously can't sing. If they've no voice then you will never teach them to sing. In a musical, it will be the lack of singing that an audience will never forgive rather than a lack of acting ability. The ability to hit the top note when it matters is vital, whereas not being a thrilling actor is forgivable.

"However, going back to *Les Misérables* and research. Trevor and I did a lot of it with the English cast even though there were only three RSC actors in it. The other members

47

of the company were mainly from musical backgrounds. In their case, the research was as much to do with making them aware, as a company, of the inherent seriousness of what we were doing as it was about actually finding things out. Still, a great deal of what we did in rehearsal did grow from what they discovered. In America it would have been a bit of a con to put another company through exactly the same research process, but we did improvisation and acting exercises with the American company and Trevor did similar things with the Australian company, just as I have since done in Japan. Japan really was massively different – quite extraordinary. I started off with acting exercises, because their traditions of theatre and theatre training are so completely different from ours. The diversity of influences on actors in Japan is considerable, both from inside the country and from the West, and there is no common method – you get everything from absolute social realism from one actor to something much more akin to Chinese opera in another! So I had to give acting exercises to unify them stylistically.

"I also had to challenge most of their social assumptions. *Les Misérables* is partly about revolution and also partly about Christianity: what is the difference between a revolution and an insurrection, and what is the true nature of Christianity? Japanese society has no profound experience of either of these things. Japan is a country which has never undergone revolution and has only a very hazy knowledge of what the history of Christianity is all about. The difference between the Old Testament idea of God and that of the New Testament – one of the main driving forces behind *Les Misérables* – is something which had to be explained to them from scratch. It's an important issue for the characters to understand. Valjean's belief is in the God of Jesus Christ, the merciful, forgiving, all-embracing God, and Javert's is in the retributive, revengeful God of wrath of the Old Testament. It was very hard for the Japanese to understand that people living in nineteenth-century France could believe that those two ideas could be embodied in one and the same God, that two people in the same society, reading the same Bible, could take completely opposing pieces of evidence to support their own view of God, and at the same time think of themselves as Christian.

"The whole production was a most challenging task. It's exciting to collide with a totally different culture – that kind of collision can produce great theatrical sparks. The actors loved the whole process from the very beginning. They are wonderful, the Japanese; so dedicated, hard-working and optimistic about getting things right. The work-ethic is very strong there. I had a hard job persuading them to take one day off a week! There was also a great deal of self-humour in the air, and silliness. Their inscrutability is skin-deep. I had real fun with them in rehearsals – constant laughter. In fact, it was one of the most scrutable companies I've ever worked with."

Having explained the problems of the Japanese actors, he was frank about his own, not least the language hurdle. "I had to learn a certain amount of Japanese in order to be able to understand the text. You cannot do any very serious work on it if you don't know what is being said. I did have the use of a marvellous interpreter. There was no other way to tackle it.

"One of the difficulties in working in Japanese was the complexity of the written language. In order to work on the score, I had to have the Japanese characters – which are actually Chinese characters! – written under the musical line and then, under these, they wrote out for me the phonetic rendering of the characters in English so that I could look at the score and recognise what was being sung. Next, under the phonetic script, I had them write out the literal translation, not in the English syntactical order but in the Japanese, so that I knew which word corresponded with which note. Finally, after all that, I wrote what it would actually mean if you put it into colloquial English.

"So I found myself thinking in triplicate in order to under-stand what was being sung. Once I started to understand the structure of the language I began realising how greatly English song-writing depends upon English grammar! Traditional lyric writing is based on the idea that you get a rhyme at the end of each line. It just so happens that Western music hits the first beat in every bar with a stress, so composers and lyricists tend to put the final rhyming word of each lyrical line on the first, stressed, beat of a bar. In Japanese most sentences end in unimportant words – prepositions and the like. Therefore at the end of each line, you find yourself with 'of' or 'to' or 'for' or 'in' always on an important stressed rhyming note. So the tune is building up to an enormous climax and instead of singing 'love' or 'soul' or 'you', the actor has to sing 'with' or 'for' . . . it really can be a bit of a problem. The other difficulty about translating into Japanese is that it takes three times longer to say something in Japanese than it does in English. So plays either have to be lengthened in order to accommodate the extra talking time, or the text cut to fit the length of the play. In order to avoid a nine-hour *Les Misérables*, I had to agree to a text which was a great deal less detailed than the English – and a great deal more vague and poetic as a result."

Is it easier directing in the language of another Western European country, then? "Not necessarily. Shakespeare in translation causes problems anywhere because English uses more words than almost any other language. It's so rich, even without all the words that Shakespeare actually invented. This came up when I did *As You Like It* in Sweden. Swedish only has about a sixth of the words that we have in English so you have to keep re-using words that Shakespeare only used once or twice in a whole play. Swedish is perfectly good as a day-to-day language, as indeed ordinary English speech is for us, but when tackling Shakespeare's verse then you have to have a tremendously imaginative translator. I was very lucky.

"Swedish actors work in the German tradition, that is with a very long rehearsal period but very short rehearsal days and as I just didn't have that kind of time-scale I had to put them under intense rehearsal pressure and push them to do in four hours what I would, in England, have tried to accomplish in seven. The standard of acting is incredibly high, although they think that English and American actors are much, much better than they are, but this is really only because of the far greater exposure English-speaking actors get on films and television.

"They also feel that their language is a cage, that they will never be allowed out of their language, poor prisoner-cousins in the international theatre stakes. But one of the wonderful things about working on *As You Like It* in Swedish was that when it came to the first night of the play I got a much stronger feeling of what it must have been like at the very first night in 1601, or whenever it was, than I could ever have had in England. The translation was remarkably fine – Goran O. Erikson, the translator, is a real genius – and he translated it into modern Swedish. He obviously couldn't translate Elizabethan English into some kind of seventeenth-century Swedish dialect. What was remarkable was that every word was understood by the audience, and every joke was funny! To make an audience fall about listening to Touchstone's jokes is something which just never happens in England any more. As the centuries go by, poor Touchstone gets less and less funny.

"It was so liberating to hear a whole Shakespeare play spoken as if freshly written, freshly minted. Very occasionally I've had similar experiences here amongst school audiences in really out-of-the-way places where four or five hundred children have been completely on the edge of their seats because they don't want Tybalt to kill Romeo, or appalled that Juliet doesn't wake up in time to stop Romeo killing himself.

"They, too, are getting Shakespeare absolutely fresh. Much of what happens in Stratford, especially during the previews on the run-up to press night, is defined by an audience and, indeed, a profession which is saying, 'I wonder what they're going to do with it this time?' Clearly that's not an immoral response, and nobody should abandon Shakespeare because they've seen all his plays before. You can have a more profound understanding of what a play is about on a second or third or tenth encounter, but a new production should always leave room for a completely fresh and untutored view. That's something actors often have to be reminded about.

"Actors can become jaded by feeling they are playing to too many non-English-speaking tourists, or to people who have seen the play too often, or been around Stratford far too long, or just that they are playing to an overly sophisticated audience. I often have to say to the actors at Stratford, 'Stop worrying about it. Play to the hundred or so people dotted around the auditorium who have never seen a Shakespeare play before. It is quite possible, indeed probable, that in any one week of your lives you will play to at least a dozen people whose lives or perceptions will be changed in some way by the experience of watching and listening to you acting Shakespeare – and that's for *all time*. It's never going to go away from their lives. It's something they'll always remember and perhaps it will be the start of a long voyage for them, and if it is, *you* are responsible.

"'If you turn in a mediocre, unfocused, unconcentrated performance which makes them think that Shakespeare is boring, then it's *your* fault. It may be *my* fault too because of the way I have directed it. You must never expose an audience to poor acting or self-indulgent acting. You're there to expose them to Shakespeare's story and to his language and to his magic. That's why we're all here.'"

NICHOLAS HYTNER

Associate Director of the Royal Exchange Theatre, Manchester, since 1985 after directing in a number of reps. Has directed two productions for the Royal Shakespeare Company, *Measure for Measure* (1987) and *The Tempest* (1988). Credits include *Edward II* by Christopher Marlowe, *Don Carlos* by Schiller, *The Scarlet Pimpernel* by Baroness Orczy. Operas include *The Turn of the Screw*, *King Priam*, *Xerxes*, *The King Goes Forth to France*. Won Laurence Olivier Best Opera Production Award in 1986.

———————◆———————

Manchester Royal Exchange has proved to be a forcing ground for directorial talent and one of its brightest graduates has been Nicholas Hytner. He was, in fact, born in Manchester, went to Cambridge and was picked out by Jonathan Miller as Assistant Director, following a student production at the Edinburgh Festival. For such a young man his range is enormous – from Marlowe's *Edward II* to Baroness Orczy's *The Scarlet Pimpernel*, taking in Handel's *Xerxes* and the strange new opera produced at Covent Garden in 1987, *The King Goes Forth to France*, which was followed by *The Magic Flute* at the Coliseum in 1988.

"I nearly always find myself thinking of doing a play in combination with the people whom I would like to be in it, that is the best way it can be brought alive. Both *Edward II* and the more recent *Don Carlos* were totally connected with

Ian McDiarmid from the very moment we decided to do them. *Edward* was his idea and *Don Carlos* mine."

His *Edward II* was highly acclaimed, not least for the horrifying reality of the dénouement. "It's a furious and fantastic piece – not one in which there are any heroes – but it is totally courageous and therefore exhilarating and ennobling. It looks straight into the eyes of your worst fears. It seems to me that the worst fear, common to every individual, is the knowledge that the nearest you can come to bliss in this world is to experience the sort of extreme romantic passion that is ultimately destructive. It seems to me that this play had to be done because it does look extreme romantic passion in the eye, and looks at the possibility of preserving it and deepening it. That is one of the most intense of experiences and one that people hang on to as a reason for not doing away with themselves. But finally, Edward's love of Gaveston destroys England. Romantic passion and social responsibility seem mutually exclusive.

"At the end of the play I filled the stage with mud and dirt. (In reality Edward did end his days in a cell through which a sewer flowed.) It did make some people irate and provoked a passionate reaction, but that was surely the intention of the playwright. Marlowe was the great maverick of the Elizabethan stage. His was the kind of talent that had to burn out."

Tackling plays such as Schiller's *Don Carlos*, which are relatively unknown in this country, does not alarm him. "I can tell you exactly why it was important to do it. It's the personal statement of the play which is interesting to me and that is what matters. For me to be of any use to a play, I need to have a strong personal association with it, not because it can then express something about *me* but because I can think of ways of bringing it vividly alive.

"One of the main issues about being alive in this generation – although it isn't really right to generalise for my generation – is that it is now very difficult to be an idealist about anything and I think this is now common to most theatre audiences. Any play which examines the emotional traumas involved in committing yourself to a series of ideals, in fact committing yourself to anything, is vividly alive to me and that is true of both *Carlos* and *Measure for Measure*.

"Everybody in *Carlos* is involved in an intensely passionate way in a battle between what they would like to be, what they perceive themselves to be, what they would like the world to be and what they see the world as being. In virtually all great plays, people's personal traumas are echoed by political traumas, because great plays tend to be about people whose lives and actions have wider repercussions.

"I don't, however, believe that what we are doing in the theatre will bring about political change, I don't see theatre in that way, but what I do believe in is an arena in which uncertainties can be explored, sometimes even frivolously – and although it is a long time since I've done anything comic I do actually enjoy doing something just because it's funny.

"In *Carlos*, idealism, philosophical and political idealism, is the great positive but also the most destructive and dangerous element in the play. *Carlos* is perfect eighteenth-century revolutionary idealism and Schiller's own sentiments are put forward by the most eloquent character in the play and are, in fact, the seeds of his destruction. Whereas, in *Measure for Measure*, the idealism belongs to Angelo and seems tainted from the beginning; it is never presented as something which has potential nobility in it.

"When I started work on *Measure for Measure* I had in mind some lines from Yeats' poem *The Second Coming*:

> The best lack all conviction, while the worst
> Are full of passionate intensity.

That seems to me to be the most exciting thing you can put on stage. It has two sides – the worst also lack conviction and the best can have passionate intensity, but it is the first which seems to me to be apposite for now. How does passionate conviction, political or personal, turn good? How does passionate intensity combine with conviction to produce something which is best? In a sense, I'm always aware that by being so interested in a state of openness and lack of conviction, one is in danger of paralysis, as is the Duke in this particular play.

"We're all in a state of paralysis now. We have no answer to what is happening in this country. You can see, for instance, how the Labour Party is totally paralysed. The final passages of *Measure for Measure* demonstrate the absolute necessity for reconciliation. We cannot turn this into any relevant solution for 1987, but we ought to trumpet its message positively. Nobody preaches reconciliation now.

"By that, I don't mean something wet; it should never be the acceptance of the status quo, the 'we'll leave things as they are and try and get on with each other' notion. The wonderful open-eyed thing at the end of *Measure for Measure* is that the Duke has learned so much by being in the world, so much more than he knew at the beginning of the play, that he is drunk just with being alive. In fact, he sets about making things even more difficult for everyone else, although probably productively so. It seems to me at the end of the play, that the whole point is that nothing is really resolved. In the text, Isabella doesn't say whether she's going to marry him or not, she doesn't say yes or no, it's just all very difficult.

"'Love her, Angelo,' the Duke says to Angelo when he gives him Marianna, but is that possible? The question isn't answered but the point is that by the end of the play there is someone driving forward, knowing that however painful it might be for other people some of the time, he's finding his way forward towards a set of values superior to those he left Vienna to remedy and far superior to what went on in the streets of Vienna when Lucio was at large – and certainly far superior to what Angelo brought in with his new regime to try and clean it all up.

"Isabella is passionately intense about doing what is apparently the right thing, but it is very chilling. I think that at the beginning of the play there are three people – and I take Lucio as the third – who are totally certain about who they are and what their position is, absolutely totally certain. Then there is one person who is paralysed with uncertainty. None of them – with the exception of Lucio who does have moments of imagining another person's point of view – is capable of making a step outside himself towards true empathy with anyone else. That is the leap the play demands of them all.

"The process of the play is the explosion into life of the Duke who then drags everybody along with him. What you get, in effect, is the Duke having his nervous breakdown constructively and creatively and Angelo having his destructively. Angelo's breakdown leaves him with no reserves at all. I think this is also what happens to Isabella. She's fine just so long as that completely locked, hermetically-sealed image of herself is not threatened. 'Let him marry her,' she says, when she hears Claudio has made Juliet pregnant. Her ideals, her Christianity, her piety, are compromisable until events actually touch her. It is terrible. She can cope with Claudio's sexual adventures but nothing nearer to her than that.

"I do seem to have done a series of plays which appear to have a lot in common although that is not altogether true – *Don Carlos* and *Measure for Measure*, Schiller and Shakespeare, are also very much at variance with one another. I'm not interested in day-to-day plays, in mundane plays. I'm interested in expansion, in making things more intense and making them harder, more questioning, more worrying.

"That sounds like the old saying about, 'I don't want to go to the theatre to see my own front room', but I do go to see things which are essentially there inside me organised and made theatre for me. So one of the reasons that I remain committed to the Royal Exchange is because it is a place for communal hopes, fears and uncertainties – particularly communal uncertainties – to happen, that's why I love it. But I enjoy working at the RSC as well."

He has mentioned working closely with Ian McDiarmid. Does he work together with his actors to arrive at a joint idea? "I tend to bring a strong framework of ideas with me, a strong feeling for the world I think the play belongs to. If you work at all in opera, you get used to doing your homework, to being conceptually creative before you arrive in the rehearsal room. But then it is a matter of working through those ideas together, bouncing them off one another, and I like being challenged all the way through. Ian and I are both directors of the theatre in Manchester, but even there different actors demand different things. For instance, David Howey, the RSC's Provost in *Measure for Measure*, has worked with me in Manchester and he is a constantly challenging actor whose contribution to a production is always accurately observed and who always gives a careful performance, but who is constantly nudging me into avoiding the banal or frivolous solution. I find that essential.

"When I did Robert Glendenning's play *Mumbo Jumbo* and was entirely surrounded by seventeen-year-olds, I found, for the first time in my career, that the vast majority of the cast were younger than me. It was lovely and very flattering for my ego, but, in the end, I was heavily relying on those few who were older and prepared to challenge me back."

How did he feel about taking on a totally different kind of play, such as *The Scarlet Pimpernel* at Chichester and then in London? "I loved it. In a sense, almost more was at stake because more people would come to it looking for a good night out! There were parts which were good and I was really pleased with them, but there were others that weren't and made me wish I'd been much more ferocious in rehearsal. I loved Donald Sinden – mind you, if he doesn't want to take any notice, he won't, but he never says, 'Belt up!' It was his idea to ask me to do it as he's a great opera fan and had seen my production of Handel's *Xerxes* at the Coliseum. He thought someone who could do opera was a good idea for that play.

"Actually, I'm very catholic in my tastes, though I'd be a liar if I said I enjoyed only those things which imitated life. I admire productions by Howard Davies, for instance, because there seems to me to be an enormous sense of control, which is sometimes lacking in mine. He draws in, rather than pushes out, and I love to see it although I know I cannot do it myself.

"I love doing opera because music can suggest extremes of emotional language and also extremes of total harmony. It's something I'm now hooked on although I've never yet felt that I've done a really good opera production. How do I manage singers who are not good actors? I don't have to any more because I can now insist on being involved in the casting . . . Of course, it's different when you're asked abroad because your cast is provided for you. There are things I just wouldn't direct, like Wagner, for which big fatties are still required. But I've been lucky that, by and large, the operas I've done over the last four years have all been cast very well.

"The singers always have phenomenal musical imaginations which is very exciting to work with. Their job has never required them to be as theatrically imaginative as actors, so therefore the director's imagination is being more heavily relied upon. It's very interesting to be challenged by a conductor who says that the musical argument doesn't allow for this or that – that's great – but not to be challenged about the actual characterisations within the opera is sometimes stifling.

"The most important thing is to provide the right world for both operas and plays. If you don't, then the work becomes lost. I'm suspicious both of total naturalism and complete dislocation. With *Don Carlos* it would have been quite easy just to show the world of sixteenth-century Spain, but I think it should always be just one step beyond what you expect, not total dislocation or, worse still, decoration.

"One's soul should engage in an evening in the theatre. Anything that engages a sense of humour, of hope, of fear or joy, through communal imagination, is right and good and that is what we must fight for.

"This is the age of disillusion. I realise I lived very briefly through a better one, as I was at university in the mid-1970s. It was the tail end of idealism, and since then it's been flying away from us. Only recently, has one been able to express rage at having that idealism whipped away. Even worse, one looks now at an age where people are content just to be materialistic, not angry and feeling there is something missing. In the theatre, what is missing can still be provided – even if we cannot say overtly, 'This must change', because that can't happen.

"Those who come to the Royal Exchange, to Stratford, to the subsidised theatre in general, tend to be – by and large – the liberal middle classes. There is no point and, to me, something profoundly useless about seeing a bad play, however admirable its aims and political philosophy might be, and seeing it being preached at people who dare not admit it is bad or lacks soul and humanity because it is preaching something they think they should be agreeing with. That's a depressing experience. Fortunately that is happening less often now than it was a few years ago.

"It seems to me that we should be trying to provide that sense of social consensus which is now missing. When you hear Norman Tebbit say that there's no difference between page three of *The Sun* and a Titian, then you have to say that those who cannot differentiate between them are not properly alive. We must, therefore, provide three hours of experience which makes people more alive and brings them more in touch with – for want of a better word – their own spirituality."

BILL ALEXANDER

Associate Director of the Royal Shakespeare Company. Started career in theatre in 1971 as member of The Other Company. In 1973 joined Bristol Old Vic, moving on to the Royal Court in 1975. On leaving the Court worked as a freelance, directing plays in Nottingham, Ipswich and Edinburgh. Joined the RSC in 1977 and productions included plays by Barrie Keeffe and Stephen Poliakoff. Shakespeare productions include tour of *Henry IV*, Parts I and II (1980), *Richard III* (with Antony Sher, 1984), *The Merry Wives of Windsor* (1985) and *Cymbeline* (1987). Winner of 1986 Laurence Olivier Award for Best Production with *Merry Wives*.

⎯⎯⎯◣◢⎯⎯⎯

Like many directors, Bill Alexander first became interested in directing when he was at university. "I was at Keele, which doesn't do an official drama course – there was no such thing – but I still spent most of my time getting together theatre groups, doing a good deal of experimenting, very much influenced by the American groups of the late sixties, like La Mama Theatre. So we formed groups based on those kinds of principles.

"When I went to London I became involved with Interaction, run by Ed Berman at Chalk Farm, which had two small theatre companies in-built into it; one was the Dogs Troup and one was TOC, The Other Company, which was run by an Israeli director. I heard that TOC, which was quite an influential company, was re-forming with a new group of actors so I went along and auditioned and got into that. The group itself had changed since its beginnings and was to become one of the two companies on the Fun Art Bus which was Ed's baby at the time.

"It was while I was acting on the Fun Art Bus with TOC that someone showed me a clipping from *The Stage*, inviting applicants for the Thames Television Trainee Directors' course so I applied and eventually got a bursary. You were seconded to a repertory theatre for two years to act as an assistant director and I went to the Bristol Old Vic. Howard Davies was also there and I assisted him on some shows and in the course of those two years ended up doing about a dozen shows myself.

"Val May was running the Bristol Old Vic then. It was a three-theatre operation with the new studio theatre which had been opened when the building was renovated, and also the Little Theatre in the Colston Hall, in which I did several productions. There were lots of opportunities.

"My very first professional production was *Butley* by Simon Gray at the Little Theatre with Paul Darrow as Butley, and John Nettles and Peter Postlethwaite were in it too. That was my initiation. In the course of the two years I did *Twelfth Night*, Noël Coward's *Blithe Spirit* with Paul Daneman and Kate O'Mara – which was Peggy Anne Wood's Golden Jubilee production – Alan Ayckbourn's *How the Other Half Loves*, with Michael Rothwell, a great favourite local actor, and several studio productions including Peter Handke's *The Ride Across Lake Constance*, followed by a one-man show with Michael Rothwell called *Notes from Underground* based on a Dostoyevsky short story – a real mix.

"I had a certain amount of choice although usually it was put before me by Val who said, 'Would you like to do this?' and I generally said yes. I don't remember doing anything I actually thought up myself. I usually waited for someone else to come up with suggestions."

Bristol was followed by a spell at the Royal Court, then came some freelancing before he finally joined the Royal

Shakespeare Company in 1977, directing a string of new plays by writers such as Stephen Poliakoff, Howard Barker and Barrie Keeffe. It was not until 1984 that he directed his first production in Stratford's main house, the now classic and universally-acclaimed production of *Richard III* with Antony Sher.

How have his working methods developed over the years, have they altered very much? "I would say essentially not, although I'm sure one's approach is changing all the time, often in ways imperceptible even to oneself. One thing I am aware of looking back is that when I started directing I was relying purely on instinct and since then I have acquired knowledge so that my work now is a combination of knowledge and instinct. I think the great danger that can befall a director, however, is if knowledge takes over completely and instinct evaporates. It is something I am terribly on my guard about.

"Unlike some directors, I have never had an applied method. I think you could say that Max Stafford-Clark at the Royal Court has a method which he constantly applies to his work, although I am sure he is always changing it and refining it. Clearly Mike Leigh also has his own method. I've never been like that and have always adapted my approach to the demands of the particular production. Sometimes I use a great deal of improvisation in rehearsal, sometimes I use none at all, it depends on the composition of the cast, the play and what one is trying to achieve.

"Sometimes I spend two weeks on a text before beginning to move it, sometimes we will begin moving the play immediately, sometimes physically. Sometimes you begin with a whole series of related exercises or with a great deal of research. It's fluid and, again, I think you are relying on your instinct for what is right in terms of the combination of the play you are trying to crack, the company you are working with, the environment in which you are doing it and where you feel you are yourself – not forgetting the audience you think you will be addressing."

A combination of the right play with the right actor creates a kind of magic, as was seen in his production of *Richard III* with Antony Sher. "Yes, I do have a very special and productive relationship with him. We're careful about doing the right things together and also that we don't do too much. We may now not work together for a year or two and only come together again when we know we've found something which is right for both of us.

"When we are working on a play in which he has a part, then it is very much thrashed out between us. He is an actor who, even more than most, brings his own ideas to the rehearsal room – there's no doubt about that – and then it's often a question of debating his ideas rather than mine. But that's marvellous, that's Tony and my relationship with him. It works. There's no question of his going right outside what I think is right, because we will have discussed the context of the play thoroughly before we began."

The first time we met he was in the middle of rehearsing *Cymbeline*, a play which is not put on very often but which has had two major productions recently, the second directed by Peter Hall at the National Theatre as part of his cycle of late Shakespeare plays. Had Bill Alexander found it a hard play to tackle?

"It's more difficult in the sense that it's a complicated play and the balance of tone in it is difficult. It has such a mixture of elements of tragedy, romance and near-comedy apart from being, in some senses, a history play as well. There are so many elements, so many different moods that one has to reconcile and blend in to each other, that there are real difficulties. It's a play which has very grittily realistic scenes of sexual jealousy, yet the same structure can contain the appearance of Jupiter on the back of an eagle, an encounter with the gods and a vision of a divine tablet, so it is, indeed, a mysterious and problematic play.

"But one of the pleasures of doing it was that when you're working on the great, the well-known, plays of Shakespeare you find yourself thinking, 'How can I do this in a different way?', knowing how it has been done before. You can always be sure that a proportion of the audience sitting out there at the performance is thinking, 'I wonder how he'll do *that* bit', knowing it's coming up in a moment. So the great thing about *Cymbeline* is that so few people know it, so it isn't a question of how will the next bit be done but of what is the next bit?

"It is also quite simply a cracking good yarn, a good story. If I hadn't read it because I wanted to do it, I'd have gone to see it out of curiosity if someone else had been putting it on, in order to be surprised. It bucks you up all the time knowing that you're dealing with surprises, which was the original intention, of course, when Shakespeare wrote it. One of the very real problems about doing Shakespeare now is that that kind of reaction is pretty hard to come by."

His production of *Cymbeline* was put on at Stratford's Other Place, which he felt a definite plus. "Directing Shakespeare for The Other Place is easier in many ways in the sense that you have far greater flexibility of tone. This particular play is difficult enough without struggling with doing it on the big main stage.

"The sense of 'here we go again, we've seen it all before' is something I felt all too strongly with both *The Dream* and *Twelfth Night* and that can be very daunting. Funnily enough, I did not feel like that with *Richard III* because, in a way, it is not such a well-known play."

This led on to the subject of the relationship between director and designer and William Dudley's designs for *Richard* were very striking indeed. "Over the years, Bill and I have done a lot of good work together and it's been a productive relationship, although we are now going our separate ways. The plays I did with Bill in the main house – *Richard III* and *Merry Wives of Windsor* – were great fun and then we'd go and do something really austere in The Other Place as a kind of recanting process. It was absolutely wonderful. With Nigel Williams' *Country Dancing* (a play about Cecil Sharpe and folk music) there wasn't really a set at all, only costumes, yet we'd come straight to that from a production of *The Dream*."

His production of *Merry Wives* won him a string of awards.

Set in the 1950s – which raised some initial doubts, not least in this writer – it proved both a critical and a commercial success. Did he choose that period because he felt there were difficulties again with such a well-known play?

"Actually, I'd question whether it is that well known. Certainly Terry Hands' 1970 production became very well known but not the play itself. It isn't put on all that often. Why did I set it in the 1950s? Because that period seemed to suit it so well. The play's about an England which was prosperous, relaxed, nostalgic, in which there was a clash of classes – the aristocracy and country people and the *arriviste* new rich.

"There are great similarities between the late Elizabethan-early Jacobean age and the late 1950s. It seemed to me a perfect parallel, more than any other period you could pick on. Morals were free enough for people like Falstaff to think they could get away with it, while there was also the incomprehensibility of what the new upward social mobility meant to women of working-class origin – actually, they would be the last people on earth to be seduced by an old aristocrat and this was exactly what Shakespeare was writing about. Also, it's the only play of his which is really about the middle classes instead of lords and ladies and the aristocracy. So, again, the fifties' setting was appropriate to a period when our own aristocracy was still quite affectionately regarded, as is the main character in *I'm All Right Jack*, but where they were no longer in a position of power.

"In fact, what I had really wanted was that when Ford ripped aside the curtain to try to find Falstaff it would reveal that huge poster of Macmillan saying 'You've Never Had It So Good!', as a way of increasing Ford's sexual jealousy and with the poster facing outwards so that people could read it. No, I was never in any doubt that setting it in the fifties was the right idea."

As he says, though, there are real problems for any director tackling Shakespeare's well-known plays. "You're not just handed them to do as you are when you are young and not established, and for some time now I have been able to choose what I want to do, but I did feel daunted by *The Dream*. It becomes a matter of going over all the previous marvellous productions, like Peter Brook's, and you tell yourself it's a wonderful play, a great opportunity, but I found that in my case my heart just wasn't totally in it."

He did not feel like that about *The Merchant of Venice* in which Antony Sher played Shylock. His production brought out the fundamental unpleasantness of the play and the appalling nature of most of the characters. It played in tandem at Stratford with Christopher Marlowe's *The Jew of Malta* which was on at the Swan. "I don't think you can doubt the nastiness of the people; you can't duck it. It's the way you explain Shylock's behaviour for if you duck it he becomes a simple villain. If the Christians are nice people then you don't understand why he is as he is. If they are as bigoted and unpleasant as I think Shakespeare intended them to be, then his behaviour becomes, if not forgivable, then at least entirely comprehensible.

"To me, Bassanio is a feckless, rather spineless individual who certainly doesn't deserve anyone as good as Portia – but then who can tell what any woman's taste is? Or a man's, for that matter: it's a mystery. Not that I think Portia's a terribly pleasant character either, so perhaps they deserve each other. Some people objected to the way I saw Portia, feeling she should be shown as just beautiful, gracious, poetic and brave but I felt that was sentimentality. People want heroines out of Mills and Boon rather than real people and I really liked the Portia in my production. She was part of that corrupt world of Venetian society and even if she did live out in the country it didn't make her a paragon of virtue. She's brave but also a nuisance. Brave people are often quite unpleasant in real life and nice people are often not at all brave."

After a busy 1987–8 Stratford season he took a year off from productions to run the RSC in London, "because I desperately needed a change from all that directing. I'd done eight major productions in two years and in 1987 alone I had put on three main house productions on the run, followed by

Cymbeline in The Other Place. This meant that for a whole year there were only five or six weeks when I wasn't actually in rehearsal. The break has been very valuable."

When I saw him next he was clearing out a mountain of old paperwork. "I come in here at about ten o'clock and tear up memos every day – it's quite therapeutic. I'm very much enjoying quietly running things here at the Barbican. It's true that a change is as good as a rest. I'm really not pushing myself to think of what I want to do next and trying to put ideas out of my mind, although there is a play now which I really do want to direct and that is Webster's *The White Devil* which I'm now beginning to work on.

"Apart from that, I'm reading through the whole Shake-speare canon again. I feel very centred on the Shakespearean and Jacobean repertoire at the moment. It would be wrong for me to shift off that and say it's time I took a break because I've done a lot of it; the whole of the early part of my career was spent directing new plays and it really is only in the last five years that I've tackled the great plays. It's too fundamental a thing to try to be good at, to say, oh I've done enough of this kind of theatre so it's time I did a new play, or a Chekov, or a modern American classic. I really want to get to grips with the Shakespearean repertoire and the plays of his contem-poraries. I feel I've only touched the surface of it and I have a long way to travel."

The other task he set himself for his year in London was to try to keep the company together as it is when it is based in Stratford, and that is far more difficult when the actors become scattered in London. "Every time we've moved to London in the last five or six years, we've lost cohesion in some way and this is something I've been conscious of want-ing to correct.

"I wanted to be able to maintain an objectivity about the whole organisation and to respond at any time to what is going on, look after the company's health at all levels – organising understudy rehearsals, workshops, re-examining aspects of my own work throughout the year. You have to be alert to every nuance of company spirit. Maintaining that

spirit is a natural process in Stratford where a good company
of actors is bound together by the geography of the place; it's
harder keeping that spirit when the company is in London
and there is a diffusion of energy. I've felt my main task has
been to maintain the company's imaginative life and keep its
sense of activity going."

Following criticism about the speaking of Shakespearean
prose and verse by the RSC, the company's actors in both
London and Stratford have had workshops on acting and
speaking Shakespeare. "I think it's extremely important to
address ourselves to the techniques and styles required for
acting Shakespeare in a large space. I also felt the need for
workshops on verse in relation to character; how the playing
of a part must not be allowed to inhibit the intrinsic qualities
of the verse; how rhetoricism has to be avoided but how, in
avoiding it, you can help form character from outside the
individual actor's interior speculation about how that character should be played."

Overall he feels the London season has been a good one.
"The actors are optimistic although some are disappointed
there has not been new work for them. On the whole, the
shows have gone well; the press has been good, the audiences
are coming and we're entering an exciting phase with this
company's new work." This has included a departure, a short
season at the Almeida Theatre, which is something he wanted
to do in London. "The Almeida season is liberating because
it has allowed us to do work we could not have done in The
Pit and has given the actors another outlet in what I think is
one of the best spaces in London.

"Often the new pieces of work you do in this second year
have the benefit of the company having been together for
quite a while, working in a very integrated way. That shows
in John Barton's production of *The Three Sisters*. But the
second year is difficult because what are you preparing for?
You aren't preparing to launch off into some brave new
future; you can't offer them ten-year contracts. But I feel this
is one of the best companies we have had for a long time and
I will be pushing for what I have consistently said is necessary;

that it will be held together and go back to Stratford looking very much as it is now. Then we'll really have something to build on."

HOWARD DAVIES

Started work as Associate Director at Bristol Old Vic. Worked in fringe theatre and repertory before joining the Royal Shakespeare Company as an Associate Director. Credits include *Long Day's Journey into Night* by Eugene O'Neill, *Bingo* by Edward Bond, *Macbeth*, *Troilus and Cressida*, *Les Liaisons Dangereuses* by Laclos (latter three RSC). Joined the National Theatre in 1987 where productions have included *Cat On A Hot Tin Roof* by Tennessee Williams and *The Shaughraun* by Dion Boucicault.

———————◆———————

It was hardly possible to go to London during 1987–8 without seeing advertisements for Howard Davies' production of *Les Liaisons Dangereuses*. An unlikely subject for a play, adapted as it is from a French eighteenth-century epistolary novel by Laclos, it has been an enormous success both in this country and in New York. The man behind it is soft-spoken and modest but has obvious tenacity – obvious because he needed it to become a director in the first place.

"My first four years in the theatre were spent in stage management and they were not happy. I didn't train for that. I did a post-graduate course at Bristol University which was supposed to teach you about directing, but it was absolutely useless because it was largely taught by academics who had never worked in the theatre. So I kept on booking the theatre there and when people asked me what I was booking it for,

I'd say, 'I don't know, I'll work that out later.' I just kept putting on plays.

"I was very hard up. I'd had to borrow money to go there as I couldn't get a grant, and when I finished I found I couldn't get work because most of the Thames' training schemes for young directors in the theatre were given to Oxbridge people who were able to talk themselves into the job. So I went into stage management in the hope I might still get into directing, but there is no recognisable route. First I went to Birmingham Rep and then back to Bristol.

"It was four years before I was finally given a touring production and then Val May offered me a production in the main house – Edward Bond's *Narrow Road to the Deep North*. I don't know why he took the risk. The risk was with me rather than in putting on the play, for May was doing a lot of adventurous work at that time and in that context I don't think *Narrow Road* was seen as being particularly controversial or a threat to the reputation of the theatre. The Old Vic was being renovated and the company had moved to Bath so all this was staged in Bath.

"I suppose you can say I did come in the hard way – at least, it wasn't made easy and I was living on nothing. The production was critically well received and then I lied and said I'd three offers of jobs, as I couldn't face going back to being a stage manager. They took me on as an associate director to avoid losing me although, in fact, nobody had offered me any jobs at all.

"Val May let me run a series of what were then late-night events, hiring in things from the fringe, such as Portable Theatre, and also putting on plays of our own and eventually I ran the Old Vic Studio Theatre in Bristol. I found myself arguing more and more with Val May but it was quite an enjoyable time because he let me do a lot of work.

"I learned directing by doing it. In my first year as a director at Bristol I did ten productions in nine months, including Eugene O'Neill's *Long Day's Journey into Night*, *Troilus and Cressida* and Frank Wedekind's *Spring Awakening*. I would open a production on a Thursday night and go into rehearsal with the next one the following Monday. Most of the plays were picked by Val May and he was very good at that. I wasn't really part of the planning process and policy making. I was consulted, but I didn't instigate it. Anyway, I had no time at all to go to meetings. He was obviously using my hunger for work – I had a four-year backlog of things I wanted to do. I did make a lot of suggestions and I had wanted to do *Long Day's Journey into Night*.

"The repertory system means that you put a play on with three and a half weeks of rehearsal. Initially I suppose I learned very old-fashioned methods of working: to block it over the first two days and then try to investigate the play which, in reality, meant trying to get the actors off the script within eight or nine days. I remember doing Edward Albee's *Who's Afraid of Virginia Woolf?* with Stephen Moore and Rowena Cooper and we had a run-through of the play after four days. That was the system and you couldn't escape it because the turnover is so fast. I was extremely lucky with my actors – for instance, I had Paul Eddington as the father in *Long Day's Journey into Night* and Anna Calder-Marshall as Cressida.

"So I wasn't dealing with people who were just beginning; I had experienced and talented actors from whom I could learn. It was rather hard on them to have me. I did have some terrible rows with actors who didn't want to be told what to do by an upstart kid who'd only done four months' work on directing in his life.

"I was happy to have the arguments in a way because they helped me formulate what I was doing. Finally, though, I resigned from the Old Vic. As I wanted to do some new work, I'd commissioned a play which another associate director considered obscene. He persuaded Val May to censor it. When Val May asked me to cancel the show on the grounds that it was obscene, I refused, which left me with no alternative but to resign. They put up notices saying the play shouldn't be seen by people under the age of eighteen and, of course, it sold out . . .

"Immediately after I resigned I was picked up by Buzz Goodbody. I had put on a drama documentary based on the

Oz trial, as soon as the trial had finished. It was compiled by a friend of mine who is now dead, David Illingworth, and it was done first as a late-night show. Buzz saw it and wanted it for The Place in London where she was doing a season for the RSC, and I got to know her through that. She'd seen several productions of mine and I was hoiked up to London for an interview with the RSC to become an assistant director, which I actually didn't want to do. I wanted to direct, not sit on someone else's shoulder; I'd done enough of that as a stage manager.

"But I was in a difficult position. My wife had just had our first child, I was out of work and we'd no money coming in, so although I was very loath to take the job, I accepted it. I actually tried to put conditions on the RSC, like would they let me do a production of my own the next year? I don't know why they took me after all that, but they did. So I assisted John Barton and David Jones and I did a not-very-good production of a Snoo Wilson play as well as productions in Wales and Birmingham. Then I left the RSC.

"Immediately Trevor Nunn contacted me and very gener-ously said he could understand why I didn't want to be an assistant director but would I like to come back and do two productions? One was Bertolt Brecht's *Schweik in the Second World War*, the other Eugene O'Neill's *The Iceman Cometh* at the Aldwych. I think Trevor was very bold to let me do these. By then I was beginning to understand how the RSC worked. It's a gargantuan organisation.

"Trevor then asked me to join the company as a director but I told him I couldn't. I didn't see myself as a Shakespeare director. I couldn't trust myself with Shakespeare as it didn't feel right for me, but if he were to set up a new-play policy I would love to run that. For six months I heard nothing at all. Then Trevor came back: the silence was not because he wasn't interested but because he had been struggling with the board and the Arts Council and everyone thought the best way was to find a permanent building where that kind of work could go on in London, as an adjunct to the Aldwych. Would I a) find it (which was no small problem) and b) run it? It was a scary challenge." The result was the founding of The Warehouse in Covent Garden.

How much had his working methods changed by that time? "The luxury of working within the RSC meant that I had six or seven weeks' rehearsal and I could explore the text in many different ways. It was no longer just a matter of intellectually analysing the lines or trying to discover what you felt were the emotions contained in them. I had a deep resistance to the kind of loose improvisational techniques used by many people working on the fringe in the different disciplines, whether drama or dance. They might be useful exercises for a warm-up but they had begun to be seen as a way of rehearsing instead of as an adjunct to it, and I didn't like that. In rehearsal I tended to work out exercises or exploratory projects which would fit the specific work I was engaged on.

"In the case of a play like Cecil Taylor's *Good*, which is so fragmented in form, it became apparent after a short period of rehearsal that we would have to talk about that dirty word, 'style'. People had very different ideas on style and we were able to spend days on what it meant, on whether it could help the play, and, if it did, what we would choose to be *our* style. It meant I had the time to explore such avenues which came out of a more rigorous approach to the play and what I wanted to do with it, an awareness that there were options, instead of being committed to an avenue of thought from day one of rehearsal because the schedule meant that you couldn't possibly change your mind.

"So I suppose I found my own way because I'd never been a real assistant director to anyone. I used to bunk off when I was supposed to be working with John Barton, not because I didn't like him but because I couldn't work in that way. As I've never sat at anyone's knee, I always felt I had to invent my own method of rehearsal.

"I also learned a lot just by talking to other directors and as the RSC was so strong I learned from the actors. The biggest change in me is that I have shifted away from *mise-en-scène* because my liking and trust of actors has just grown and grown. Earlier on I was much more flamboyant as a director, more interested in effect. I wanted to show off. I wanted it to be all about *my* production. The pleasure of working with actors now is actually exploring the problems as a group."

So to *Les Liaisons Dangereuses*. If someone actually came to a director with an idea for a play based on such a novel, surely it was unlikely they would ever get a commission? "It was Christopher Hampton's idea and I think he'd had it at the back of his mind for quite a while. I'd wanted to do his play *Tales from Hollywood* as there was a fight going on at the National as to who would direct it and it was constantly being postponed. I rang him and asked him if we could do it at the RSC instead and offered him a wonderful cast, but although he was very tempted he stayed loyal to the National. So I asked him to write a play for us. He said he had no idea what to write but that he could adapt something.

"So then I had to tackle Laclos' book which I found impossible to read. It was a bad translation, it took me ages and the whole project nearly disappeared. I found a better translation but even so I told Chris I didn't see how it could possibly work. He was very cross and said, 'Well, if that's your attitude I'll go away and do it anyway!'

"When he came back he handed me a script which was like a film or television script. 'There are about eighteen different locations here,' I objected, 'boudoirs, houses and so on, and I'm going to be doing it at The Other Place which is not a theatre with scenic devices.' 'That's your problem,' he replied. He found it very funny because I'd been so sceptical about *his* talent and now he was saying, 'Well, show me yours.'

"That was another play where the question of style and form was all important. We'd a lot of argument about it in rehearsal because I didn't want anyone to use a prop or a cane: I didn't want it to be eighteenth-century in that sense. The language is really Oxford in the thirties; it reads like *Glittering Prizes*, very witty and quite lethal. We discussed it and decided that the only means of production for the characters in the play was their language. We had to concentrate absolutely on how they spoke to each other, in what manner; the power games they played were exactly to do with that and nothing else.

"Also we made it very English. People hardly touched each other. Again, there was a great deal of discussion as to how sensual it should be. I said the English sensibility regarding sexuality is very strange anyway: they see sex as tragic or farcical but not something to be engaged in directly or whole-somely, so the way to do it was to be very English, hardly going into each other's arms. By holding it all back, the sexuality became contained in a fettered way and I think was more powerful for that. We were faced with numerous choices and I think, by and large, we made the correct ones."

In spite of his earlier feelings about Shakespeare, when his time at the Warehouse came to an end he went to Stratford where, as well as the Laclos, he directed three Shakespeare productions. He feels he failed on *Macbeth*. "There's no sub plot but it's a very difficult play to get around and although I had a good company of actors, I didn't make it work: I still don't know why. Then I tried again with *Henry VIII* and I couldn't make that work either.

"I wanted David Edgar to work on it with me because it's a bastard script, parts of it were written by Shakespeare and parts by somebody else. I felt it was an old playwright working with a young one, and it varies from the terrible to very good. I said to David, 'Why don't you re-write the poor bits so that we can stay with the Shakespeare, but would it become a Shakespeare and Edgar play?' I didn't feel people would grieve too much because it was only *Henry VIII*. In the end, I don't think he could quite bring himself to do it. He stayed in rehearsals and was invaluable and did re-write scenes which we rehearsed, and that was very exciting, but he just felt he didn't have the courage to be that impertinent. So the final result was a disappointment to me because there was such a disparity between what I'd wanted to do and what I achieved.

"Finally, I plucked up courage to have a third go. When I told Trevor I wanted to do *Troilus and Cressida*, he tried to get me to direct *Merry Wives* as he had planned that Bill

Alexander should do *Troilus*. In the end, Bill and I did a swap. Trevor thought I was just making life difficult for myself but I had a very strong idea. I felt by pushing it as hard as I could it didn't become intrusive, because by setting the play in the Crimean War it is actually, geographically, near to the original anyway. I also thought the Crimea was the last of the romantic wars and it was only when people began to read *The Times*' reports that they woke up to the fact that it was a dreary mess, not a romantic escapade."

Howard Davies is one of the many bright theatrical talents who have marched over Waterloo bridge to join the Richard Eyre regime at the National Theatre. A successful production of Tennessee Williams' *Cat on a Hot Tin Roof* was followed by what seemed a most unlikely play for Davies, Dion Boucicault's nineteenth-century comedy-melodrama, *The Shaughraun*. The text had come into his hands by chance from a friend of his Henry VIII, Richard Griffiths. "I didn't look at it for months and only when I was asked for it back did I finally read it and just fell in love with it.

"But I didn't dare do it at the RSC; somehow it didn't seem right. Also I'd been so associated with plays by people like Edward Bond, really difficult, serious plays. It was a constant joke at the RSC that I couldn't direct comedy. I was frightened that if I put it up someone would take it away from me, like a child having a comic ripped out of its hands. So I sat on it.

"When I came to the National I showed it to Peter Hall and Richard Eyre and they both loved it. I had a moment of sheer panic and told them they'd better find another director as I couldn't do it. But they were remorseless and insisted that I did." The production received rave reviews and was delightful in that it was presented absolutely straight, in spite of the no doubt great temptation to send it up. "I was quite definite that I wanted Stephen Rea for the main part too. I know it's a kind of insecurity when a director says, 'I must have this one actor and no other', but I knew he would be exactly right and he was."

For the future, there is a new David Hare play, which the

author does not want to direct himself this time, "he doesn't want to do that any more". Howard Davies will be part of a small policy-making group which assists with the choice of repertoire for the National. Guest directors will be brought in, as will young directors who will be given a chance to work within the system, because working for such a huge organisation as the National presents its own problems. "It's an administrative task as well as a creative one. You need the sheer technical know-how to make something work and you can't get that by working on the fringe, however valuable the work you've done."

Compared to regional reps, directors working at the National do have long rehearsal periods but still nothing like the time allowed to theatres on the Continent. "That requires a proper level of state funding. You can't rely on sponsorship from private enterprise. Also, with private sponsorship, inevitably comes a desire to restrict what is put on. During a Sponsors' Evening at a preview of *The Shaughraun* I was introduced to one of the leading figures in Nestlés, and he fulminated against the play, saying that the National Theatre shouldn't be doing work like that at all. So bang goes sponsorship from Nestlés, which may or may not be a good thing, but if one is dependent on it and is running a theatre, then that kind of response could be very alarming."

Like virtually every other director interviewed in this book, he looks to the future of arts funding, therefore, with apprehension.

MICHAEL BOGDANOV

Directed, produced and wrote for television after leaving Trinity College, Dublin. Worked with Peter Brook as Associate on the famous production of *A Midsummer Night's Dream*. In 1971 became Associate Director of the Tyneside Theatre Company in Newcastle and in 1973 Artistic Director of the Phoenix Theatre, Leicester. Became Artistic Director of the Young Vic in 1978. Worked for the Royal Shakespeare Company and the National Theatre. Credits include (for the RSC) *The Taming of the Shrew* (1979) for which he won the Director of the Year Award, and *Romeo and Juliet* (1986). For the National, where he became an Associate Director, his credits include *The Romans in Britain* by Howard Brenton, *Uncle Vanya* by Anton Chekov, *The Caucasian Chalk Circle* by Bertolt Brecht, *Lorenzaccio* by Alfred de Musset and *The Spanish Tragedy* by Thomas Kyd. Has also worked extensively abroad especially in West Germany. In 1986, with actor Michael Pennington, founded the English Shakespeare Company.

One of the few encouraging aspects of theatre in Britain today is the emergence of two major new companies, the English Shakespeare Company founded by Michael Bogdanov and Michael Pennington and the Renaissance Theatre Company, the brain child of actor Kenneth Branagh. Both have proved that, in spite of popular belief and dismal forebodings, there is a large audience for Shakespeare outside London both in this country and all over the world.

The English Shakespeare Company now has all Shakespeare's history plays (apart from the somewhat maverick *King John*) in its repertoire which is an achievement by anybody's standards. Michael Bogdanov, the son of a Russian father and Welsh mother, has come a long way, yet he still has roots in Wales. "I moved to Bath so that I could be mid-way between London and Wales and I still have a cottage there. It's a preparatory move eventually to living there permanently.

"Though, in a way, I'm rootless. I was actually born and brought up in Ruislip. Then I spent ten years in Dublin so I suppose you could say I became surrogate Irish. But I can suddenly be reminded of my Welsh ancestry. My mother died recently and relations turned up from South Wales (and my mother was one of twelve) and I realised for the first time that 'Auntie Van' was Auntie Myfanwy, and then a David Lloyd George Rees turned up . . . Suddenly I found the Welshness coming out in me as I was surrounded by hundreds of Welsh cousins, aunts and uncles and there is something in me that's a cross between the Russian and the Welsh. I cry a lot, I'm very sentimental and I sing. But perhaps if you put me down in France, I'd look French."

Had he ever wanted to do anything else? "It's hard to say. When I was at school I wanted to do all sorts of things in the theatre. I used to act a lot and then I went to college and used to write with Terry Brady* – I wrote with him for six years, revues and musicals – but then I directed something and realised I could apply a good, objective, critical faculty to plays in that way and so I gradually directed more and more while I was in Ireland and finally ended up doing that."

He actually read French and German for his degree, not the most obvious choice for a director, but "I've two productions running in Hamburg at the moment so it's been very useful. There's a production of *Julius Caesar* and a children's play based on Goethe's poem, 'Reynard the Fox', which is rather like the shows I've done in this country – Longfellow's

* Terence Brady, playwright, novelist and actor. Often writes with his wife Charlotte Bingham.

MICHAEL BOGDANOV

Hiawatha, Coleridge's *The Ancient Mariner* and the medieval poem of *Sir Gawaine and the Green Knight*. From time to time I get the urge to do a piece for children. They're always presentational pieces of myths or legends or poems. I think I want to do one in Canada next year: I've been invited to put something on at a festival there, so I thought again of a children's piece. I keep trying to renew my energy in that way."

Bogdanov's career has been remarkably varied. From Ireland he went to the Tyneside Theatre Company as Associate Director, then to the Phoenix Theatre in Leicester as Director before becoming Director of the Young Vic in 1978 and directing a wide range of plays for both the Royal Shakespeare Theatre and the National Theatre. It was his production of Howard Brenton's *The Romans in Britain* for the National which resulted in the notorious prosecution by Mary Whitehouse, from which he finally, and after much anguish, emerged the victor. Significantly, the climate has changed for the worse since then with the passing of Clause 29 in the Local Government Bill.

The original idea for a touring company was considerably more modest than what has finally emerged. With Michael Pennington, who had grown weary of the increasing bureaucracy of the RSC, he had thought about putting on a small touring show and went to the Arts Council to discuss funding. To their amazement the Arts Council said the idea was too limited. It was in the area of touring large-scale plays, especially Shakespeare, that a gap existed. They would put up some of the money but the two Michaels would have to find the rest. After more discussion, they decided to begin with the two parts of *Henry IV* and then go on to *Henry V*, but raising the money was far from easy and it came from all kinds of quarters, including the Canadian owner of the Old Vic, Ed Mirvish, and the Allied Irish Bank.

This makes him uneasy. "I don't believe in this mixed economy of the arts. Unfortunately, it was the only way of getting the project off the ground, but this type of funding leaves you vulnerable to censorship from the sponsoring body and because such funding can disappear at the sponsor's whim, it is never possible to plan properly for the future."

Nor was it easy to find an opening venue and he is grateful to Roger Redfarn of the Theatre Royal, Plymouth, who gave the company its start. "Trying to get a number of English theatres to put up the necessary level of guarantee or to excite them with a cycle of seven history plays, is very difficult. They tend to say, 'Oh, can't you just do *Richard III*?' Or, 'Well, I've been offered this two-handed version of *No Sex Please in Your Trousers* and I think I might prefer that'."

The production of *Julius Caesar* at the Schauspielhaus in Hamburg was particularly popular with younger audiences because it was in modern dress, a frequent hallmark of Bogdanov Shakespeare. He has been described, variously, as an iconoclast, as crude, as over-opinionated and lacking in subtlety, but also as one of the most innovative, imaginative and energetic forces in British theatre today. Shakespeare must, for him, be accessible.

"The kind of theatre I try to create through Shakespeare is one of accessibility, one that doesn't take anything for granted. You start from the premise that nobody's seen or read the plays before – Shakespeare frequently takes that standpoint because he often tells you the story over and over again. *Richard II* is roughly set in the Regency period, the two parts of *Henry IV* and *Henry V* in an era not unlike that of the 1914–18 War, coming through the *Henry VI* (the plays being cut and arranged in three parts) to a Fascist *Richard III*."

I had expressed the opinion that no doubt the modern production of *Julius Caesar* struck home in Germany, and then went on to say that things were pretty unbelievable in this country now.

"Absolutely unbelievable here. That's why we're doing these seven plays now: the analogy is so strong. The plays deal with civil strife, conflict between Westminster and the provinces, north versus south, a ruler going off to a foreign war to avoid the problems at home. The plays cut across all kinds of politics and systems that still exist in this country – like the Irish problem. The Falklands conflict united the country in exactly the same kind of jingoistic way *Henry V* chose to unite his people against France. There are great parallels to be made."

One thing is certain; you would never mistake a Bogdanov production as having been directed by anyone else. Does he, therefore, accept much input from his actors? "A tremendous amount, actually. Of course, I provide the framework, the lasso for the project, a main line, but there are a thousand routes between A and B and you can take any one of them. However, if you only have thirteen weeks' rehearsal for seven plays then what I have been able to do – and I think this is why the company has such a strong identity – is to set an idea going and then leave a group to develop it while I go on to another group. It's rather like playing twenty chess games at the same time and moving around the room making a move on each board.

"What that means is that the company has a stake in, and a responsibility for, what they do on stage. Nobody can pass the buck and nobody can avoid that responsibility. Everyone knows what they are doing, why they are doing it and where they are going. That common ideology in a company and common identity is absolutely essential for the success of a venture like this, so therefore they've had a terrific stake in what happens and rightly so. They've got to perform for two years and are going to have an identity as a company and as actors, so they have got to be challenging themselves all the time and I've tried to pass that responsibility on to them.

"I know I wouldn't mistake these productions for anyone else's, I realise that. I know that to be true. But I think you'd find that the company would maintain that they've had terrific freedom to work and develop – for some of them too much; they would have preferred more help, stronger guidelines. But that's the inevitable consequence of having such a short time to rehearse. Nor do they have much time to run them in.

"What happens is that sometimes you have three weeks between performances of one particular play. You resuscitate it for one performance and then it's another two weeks before you do it again. You don't have the chance to bind it together, so that it's in that frustrating stage when you can't get a run at anything or consolidate it. Everything has to happen in your head because it can't happen on stage. Most plays need two or three weeks to settle in; that's the great argument for previews.

"An instant performance is not really what theatre's about. Although theatre only happens at the time, the day, it takes place, the audience is only the fourth stage of the development of a play. It gets written, it gets rehearsed, nowadays there's the technical stage – costumes, props, lighting, sound – and then the next twenty-five per cent is the audience and then it changes again. It changes all the time. Once it's in front of an audience, the audience tells you what's wrong, what's right, what's good and bad, and you act accordingly. You can cut, you can add, you can re-emphasise a performance, because nobody gets everything right in rehearsal or even in performance, but at least you can see, in relation to an audience, if something is working or not, if a piece of theatre is good or bad. So, therefore, what these shows lack at the moment is that sense of continuity."

But the company, working in this way, is, he says, indefatigable, "I've never seen a company like it. They now have this enormous strength and commitment and sense of fun. We have fun together because we all respect each other's work."

As for that special appeal to young people, "It upsets me greatly when I'm accused of messing about with the text and re-writing it. Someone who came to interview me recently said, 'Have you changed it all?' I asked her what she meant and she said, 'Well, he didn't write all that, did he?' I said, 'Of course he did.' I swear I do not change the lines, though I cut sometimes. Nobody wants to sit for five hours through *Richard III*; they complain it's still too long at three and a half hours, yet when I say I've cut it they say, 'How shocking, you should never cut the plays.'

"So I do try to speak directly to an audience that says it doesn't like Shakespeare and hardly ever goes to the theatre, but I also think it is very important to reach those hardened theatregoers, deeply entrenched, and change their attitude, and I have a wealth of complimentary letters from older theatregoers. We even have some groupies who follow us around on Saturdays and they saw every Saturday performance we did last year. People who previously have only seen Shakespeare presented conventionally have written to say they have never been so excited by a production. I don't want to claim credit for it, but it is helpful to have evidence that we are reaching people; without that evidence, it would be absolutely hopeless and I'd give up tomorrow.

"And that's even been the case with *Henry V* when an audience has suddenly been presented with a group of British yobs who have gone over the Channel to kick the shit out of people who really are pretty ill-equipped to deal with them."

He then returned to the present position in this country. "We truly are passing through an horrendous period. It's all going to get much worse before it gets any better. I do feel that the 'liberal sandwich' which occurred when some of us were growing up in the fifties and sixties, is now being squeezed by both ends, below and above, and I don't think our fightback has been nearly strong enough. This is a philistine government – it's an era of new brutalism – and you cannot imagine any of them going to the theatre, a concert, a ballet, an art gallery or anything to do with entertainment. Clauses 28 and 29 are merely symptoms of this.

"I don't think they'll go for the classics, like Marlowe. It will just be more difficult to get a new book published or a new play put on. Action will be surreptitious. It's been going on for years in an underhand way and some local authorities have banned all kinds of things.

"To return to the Elizabethans and Jacobeans. We easily forget that Shakespeare was writing in a very dangerous era. The two factions were ranged up solidly against each other and he had to walk a very precarious tightrope to avoid being arrested or worse. People tend to forget that when they say he was some kind of Elizabethan propagandist. They don't look for the hidden insurrection in Shakespeare, which is there, undercover, all the time. He removes events from the Elizabethan era and sets them in Rome or Athens and usually the reason for that is because he is writing about people he dislikes intensely. If he hadn't been that careful he might well have ended up dead."

As to the future? The Schauspielhaus would like him on some kind of permanent basis ("and they have a budget of £12 million a year, not even counting heating and telephones"), and he wants to continue doing "children's theatre, and some theatre in the street. I wouldn't want to devote myself to nothing but musicals, but I'm going to do *Shogun* and I wouldn't say no to the kind of returns some of the musicals have made! I'd be pleased to do a show that actually supported me for a bit. Sometimes it seems to be assumed that the kind of thing I'm doing now is all I've ever done, yet that's not true; during those first years in Tyneside I did everything from *The Cherry Orchard* through *Threepenny Opera* to *Antigone*, along with TIE [Theatre in Education] and street theatre – and with some of the company who are with me now.

"I like working with a company, with people I know. I don't like changing all the time. It's good for the energy to have an infusion of new thinking and talent from time to time, but I believe your best work is done when you develop a group in a particular way and everyone shares a common purpose. I don't know where we'll take the company after this – it's going to be impossible to cap this as a project. The partnership with Michael [Pennington] has been a very creative one because it's founded on mutual respect and ability and we've come at it from completely different angles. He's considered to be one of the best younger classical actors coming in from the established companies and I'm the upstart outsider, always challenging the Establishment."

The New Shakespeare Company is booked solidly abroad for the next two years, at the time of writing, with continuing English tours, but it is in the United States, Canada, Hong Kong and Japan (where it will open a new theatre) that it is in greatest demand.

Bogdanov, "the Bodger" as he is known in the trade, feels that perhaps he now needs to mark time. "As I've said, I've a number of exciting offers on the cards and I have to think about which of them I want to take. My instinct at the moment is to retreat and think for about a year. I need to re-charge. I'm not sure where the future lies or what I want to achieve and how best I can do theatre. I don't think my way lies with the big national companies. I need to write something down and get some order and cohesion into what I am thinking and doing, because when you just keep working and keep talking you go in ten different directions, even if you know where you are in your head."

DECLAN DONNELLAN

Born in England of Irish parents. Read English and law at Cambridge, called to bar in 1978. With designer Nick Ormerod founded theatre company Cheek by Jowl in 1981. Has directed all company's productions including plays by Shakespeare and British premières of *Andromache* by Jean Racine, *The Cid* by Pierre Corneille and *A Family Affair* by Alexander Ostrovsky. In 1987 received *Drama* Magazine's Award for Best Director and Laurence Olivier Award for Director of the Year. Cheek by Jowl won first prize in LWT Plays on Stage Competition and 1985 Award for Most Promising Newcomer in Theatre.

"Fearless", "outrageous" and "the thinking man's Mr Crummles", are among the descriptions of Declan Donnellan that have appeared recently in discussions of his work. His background is quite unlike that of any other director currently working in British theatre for he trained for the bar, not the theatre, and became a barrister. In 1981 he gave it all up and with the designer, Nick Ormerod, founded Cheek by Jowl.

"I'd spent several years being interviewed by the reps without getting anywhere. No one would hear of employing me. So I started doing fringe things for no money, designed by Nick. We kept asking the Arts Council to come along and see them and give us some money and finally a wonderful woman, Ruth Marks, who was an Arts Council Drama

Officer came to see us. She's dead now and it's one of the tragedies of British theatre that she is not properly recognised for what she did. She was one of those remarkable women who are full of energy, and she is responsible for the existence of the small-scale and middle-scale touring circuit in this country – companies like Shared Experience, Joint Stock and Monstrous Regiment.

"She almost created us, she was so encouraging.

"You must realise that the situation with regard to Arts Council funding has been going on for years, that the lack of money isn't something which has happened just now. When Cheek by Jowl started, I remember being told that I shouldn't start a theatre company then as it would never be possible financially. One of the things Cheek by Jowl has shown me about human nature is the crashingly awful advice people are prepared to hand out.

"It's not just the arrogance of youth saying this [he is thirty-four], it's actually the wisdom of older age looking back on the last seven years. We were told, for instance, we should never try to become an Equity company because we would never have that level of funding. We had this kind of advice both from inside and outside the Arts Council.

"So for that first year we limped around Britain on a tiny grant of £6000, not paying the actors Equity rates, and it was a great artistic success and a total social disaster! The Arts Council said, 'That's fine, you must do the tour again and here's the money' and we said, 'No, we can't face it, we're giving up.' We were very confused, I suppose, about running a company. We didn't know how to handle people.

"I think at an early stage many of us suffer from a lot of sentimental ideas about all being pals together. Now I feel that attitude has brought about something of a crisis in directing, which is also sentimental – people are frightened of directing because it's bad, right-wing, authoritarian.

"'Director' has almost become a dirty word in theatre and that's wrong. I don't want a democratic relationship between the nurse and the anaesthetist and the surgeon who has to give me a brain operation. I want the hospital run on democratic lines as to who is employed and conditions and so on, but I don't want a collective decision made as to who operates on me or the operation carried out by a collective.

"Not long ago a well-known actress was telling me how well she got on with her director. She said, 'After the perform-ance, he gives me his notes and then I give him mine.' That kind of thing sounds wonderful but I do not believe it works properly in practice. Even if you have a large company where a group of directors take the decisions, it still doesn't work without someone being in overall charge, giving a sense of an artistic whole. It shows in the productions which have no overall concept and no sense of the actors all working together.

"So many of today's productions seem to have been di-rected by a committee. That has its funny side, for in Eastern Europe where so many of these people's heroes are, there is absolutely no question of democracy on the rehearsal room floor. By all means have your company run by a panel of actors and directors, if that's what you want, but once you reach the rehearsal room it must be down to one person.

"I think it's partly to do with how confused people are over socialism in this country. There's no reason why theatre should be socialist but I do believe art should be anti-Establishment."

Directing, he says, is a completely separate thing from acting; it must be. "An actor can't say to me, 'I don't see how this fits in so I won't do it' because he can't see my overall concept any more than I can say he must feel this or that, because I don't know how he's feeling. It's a completely separate thing. There's this strange amateurishness about directing now which is some kind of hang-up from the sixties."

He feels, too, that there is today almost an obsession with balance, "that a play should somehow be a microcosm of society. I don't believe myself that a play should have to be fair or objective. A play is something you go to see, that you can accept or reject, and if you direct a play it's the text you have to be faithful to.

"I remember when I directed *Pericles*, a play which has a definite role for the gods – Diana comes and saves everyone at the end – one of the actors said, 'But maybe some of us don't believe in a God or gods, so can some of us register doubt on our faces at the end?' And I found myself thinking, well, that's an interesting idea, perhaps we should try that, and I actually spent a whole weekend mulling it over. Then I thought, sod it, in this play God exists and that's the way we're going to do it.

"I think Shakespeare is so supremely objective although we kid ourselves that we can interpret him. It's fascinating if you listen to people talking about Shakespeare. They say he's a wonderful playwright, of course, but he's a complete monarchist, or apolitical, or they take *The Taming of the Shrew* and say it's a great play but it's completely sexist, and in fact what they are doing is saying something about themselves, not Shakespeare."

One member of an audience criticised him for making Lady Macbeth seem "suburban. But that's what they recognised in themselves, you see. That kind of drive for power often is suburban. Look at some of the Royal Family, the grocer's daughter . . .

"But I do feel something very frightening is happening at the moment in the way plays are presented. Maybe it is me changing or maybe it is a sign of the times but people don't like to see figures of authority portrayed as being weak on stage. People have fantasies of power, fantasies of great strength and often you have to wean actors off beautiful fantasies of what power is about.

"That's why I think some people feel happier with opera, particularly bad opera (and a lot of it is very bad indeed), because it all seems very simple, whereas it's not like that with Shakespeare."

He feels that today there is also a kind of embarrassment about talking of the necessity for art for art's sake. "You must be careful you don't end up like a trendy vicar who's too embarrassed to talk about Jesus. You are either producing works of art or you aren't.

"You must remember that your overall commitment is to entertain. You can entertain people by making them feel miserable or by making them happy, but what the audience must realise is that it is the actors' imagination which is going to carry the evening. So what we try to work on very hard in rehearsals is a total commitment to what they are doing and that is where the bulk of the work lies. I'm trying to increase the level of that commitment all the time.

"That's the whole purpose about using classical scripts – that the plays that we do are much bigger than we are and it is impossible to put it all across in two or three hours. So we don't do *The Tempest*, we do *a Tempest*, we do *a Hamlet*, because all productions are just versions as you can't let the whole play breathe in two and a half hours.

"So we use the script to entertain the audience and we try to use as much of what is in that script as we possibly can, but we're only ever going to do part of that play. We hope it will be a good part and be entertaining, and when I say we 'entertain', I mean entertain at a very profound level. So what you see if you come into a Cheek by Jowl rehearsal is me working with the actors to produce that kind of commitment on stage, trying to involve the actor's imagination like a muscle.

"It's important not only that you drop everything so as to release in the play what is outrageous and wild, but that you enable the actor to release something from inside him. I don't quite know how it happens but there comes a moment when he or she is suddenly released into performing and is able to perform in that remarkable way where you leave yourself behind and become something else. It doesn't always work but that's what I'm trying to achieve."

So far his company, ranging in numbers from eight to twelve, has performed in over two hundred towns and cities in this country, in Europe, even going as far as Brasilia, Kuala Lumpur and Alexandria. He has not been daunted by putting on plays which the major companies have never attempted, like *El Cid*. "We did it because it's an absolutely marvellous play. It's about a woman making choices between herself and the state, and like all great plays it's absolutely relevant to today because it's about issues which will always be the same. No, we weren't daunted by it.

"I think, first of all, you need to know what the play is actually about; once you do know, then you can, as it were, drop your knickers and do it. It's essential that you're completely reverential to the letter of the text but not at all reverential to the letter of the law. That's a kind of biblical thing to say, but it's important. People seem terrified of classic French plays and some of the Spanish plays. They are terrified by things like 'honour' because it's just not English, but if honour was all it was about it wouldn't be a great play. The pretext of a quarrel in a play may be 'honour' but, of course, it's really about something deeper than that and once you realise that you can fly and relax. I actually find that easier. Plays are easy to do when they are about the great issues. If they are only about their period, whether that period is 1680 or today, then they are difficult because you have nothing secure to hang on to."

Ideally he would like a larger company now, to increase the twelve actors currently in Cheek by Jowl to twenty, "to enable us to do all the plays we would like to do". He would like to attempt the whole Shakespeare canon, and "the Spanish canon . . . I think a certain amount of doubling of parts is very good and it means the actor works hard, but we are strained with twelve. I think Shakespeare originally had slightly more than twelve but it was easier because they were all men so the doubling was easier too. The Cordelia/Fool one is obvious but I think it quite possible that Orsino and Maria doubled, for instance. You could do that today but because of contemporary theatrical conventions you could only do it by making it into a point you especially want to convey.

"But I'd never want to run a huge institution or even a theatre with a studio, like many of the reps. It makes work for work's sake. We do two plays for Cheek by Jowl every year and one or two things freelance outside and that's us absolutely stretched. The idea of being responsible for a vast edifice with, say, ten shows coming in every year is something I would never want. Some people are very good at it, and if you are it's a good thing to be able to do, but it's not for me."

Like Philip Hedley at Stratford East, he is full of praise for his board. He discusses with them what he is going to do and keeps them informed, but they leave him to get on with it and to make all the artistic decisions. Suggestions from the Arts Council that the board should be enlarged and made more "representative" have somewhat alarmed him and he feels this proposal is probably due to the fact that the Arts Council itself is so institutionalised. But he also feels that the Arts Council has been generous to his company. He now gets a grant of £129,000 a year after years of sheer sweat.

When we spoke he was at work on *The Tempest* and *Philoctetes* for Cheek by Jowl before going, with Nick Ormerod, to the National Theatre to do a freelance production of Lope de Vega's *Fuente Ovejuna*. He has a great admiration for Richard Eyre and will enjoy, he says, working with other directors for a short time.

As to the future? "I see the money given to us by the Arts Council as money to indulge ourselves artistically. But when we fail to please our audiences then we should be cut and our money given to someone else. I'm being realistic. One of the terrible problems with theatre in Britain is that companies have not been allowed to die because no one wants to be seen as being hard-faced. But by not allowing old companies to die, we've not allowed new companies to be born. If the time comes when Nick and I don't want to run Cheek by Jowl any more then the company should be wound up. I can see no reason for us to appoint another Artistic Director and then go away and work somewhere else, even if the Arts Council was prepared to fund the company. I don't believe that's how it should work."

Deborah Warner

Trained as a stage manager at the Central School of Speech and Drama. Worked as stage manager at the Orange Tree and New End theatres before joining Steve Berkoff's London Theatre Group as Administrator. In 1980 formed Kick Theatre Company and is still its Artistic Director. In 1987 directed her first production for the Royal Shakespeare Company, *Timon of Athens*, following that in 1988 with *King John*. Her credits include *Woyzeck* by Büchner, *The Tempest*, *King Lear*.

———————◆———————

After seeing Deborah Warner's *King John* at Stratford's Other Place in 1988, one reviewer said that in spite of some of his misgivings about the production she was probably the finest director of Shakespeare in the country today. This remarkable accolade came at the end of five years of praise for the Shakespeare productions she had directed for her own fringe theatre company, Kick.

Yet unlike so many of the other established directors of Shakespeare, she does not come out of the high-flying Oxbridge graduate stable, nor from the ranks of the bursaried trainee directors. She is self-taught. She finds the story of her emergence as a director somewhat dull – "because, I suppose, I've lived it and I know about it and I find it hard to imagine it interesting other people" – but it is remarkable and might well give heart to those whose knowledge, ability and creative talent have been dismissed because of their lack of "academic" qualifications.

She trained originally in stage management. "To some extent it was the only thing I could do because I went straight from ordinary school to drama school. My interest in theatre had developed at sixth-form college in Oxford where I took part in undergraduate drama but I didn't know a lot about it. I knew I didn't want to act – of that I was sure – so I decided to do a stage-management course.

"It was only after a four-year cycle of drama school, followed by stage management and then working with professional actors that I began to think I'd probably like to direct, but it was all 'probably' at that stage as I actually hadn't done any – although I believe you can't really *train* to be a director.

"It was at about that time that I started my own theatre company, Kick Theatre, which happened to grow into something more permanent and bigger than I'd originally intended. I formed it, quite simply, to enable me to direct a play. At that stage it was simply a matter of getting something together – there was a two-week rehearsal period and I used people I knew from drama school along with amateur actors who were around Oxford at the time and off we went to the Edinburgh Festival. We could only do one production a year as I had to earn my living, first in stage management and then in theatre administration."

Over the succeeding years she directed *The Tempest*, *Measure for Measure*, *King Lear* and *Coriolanus*, all with Kick. The company numbered twelve, which is about the size she reckoned Shakespeare's was and she saw no reason to doubt that this was sufficient. The critical reviews of these performances are striking in their unanimity; they speak of "flawless diction", "impressive staging", "enormously impressive and deeply moving" (of *King Lear*), and while some critics had reservations over the range of ability of her actors – something which she would dispute – her plain, utterly truthful approach to Shakespeare received praise from all except the handful who thought it was yet another example of trendy Shakespeare.

"So it was back in 1983 with Kick that I started to follow a policy of a tight-knit ensemble which would work together as often as possible, considering that we had no money. We were never funded you see – forgotten, this one is! So we were only able to pay our actors when, occasionally, we had some money, such as when the British Council paid us to tour abroad. We could never afford to pay actors during rehearsal or, indeed, in the early part of the run.

"But it was a tremendous thing to do and, looking back on it now, I realise Kick taught me a lot about a particular way of working which, hopefully, develops daily and which encourages me to continue working on those principles. People keep asking me, 'What happened to Kick?' The answer is that it doesn't exist at the moment but it could do again, sometime. I am working, though, with some of the actors from Kick; they were in Stratford last year in *Titus* and others, like Brian Demeger, are currently in *King John*.

"Kick was invaluable as a means of finding a way of working on Shakespeare, a skill which developed over four years, and all done on a shoestring, on nothing. It was not only a way of working in rehearsal, it was a production style. It was very simple story-telling which is the foundation of what I aim for each time."

Her first production for the Royal Shakespeare Company, staged at the Swan in 1987, was *Titus Andronicus*. "I haven't attempted a main-house Shakespeare but I think it would be very difficult because there is so much that you can't be sure would work in there – things can, moments can, images can, but I'm not sure about a whole evening. I couldn't imagine *Titus* working in that huge theatre."

Had she chosen to make her debut for the RSC with one of Shakespeare's most difficult plays? "No, I didn't. I was asked quite suddenly, at very short notice, and in fact I'd just signed a contract to go to Sweden to do a production for their drama school in Stockholm. I was due to leave at eleven o'clock the next morning when I was rung up out of the blue and asked if I'd like to do the play at Stratford – that was at 6 pm! I managed to negotiate myself out of the Swedish contract and accepted the job. Fortunately, I'd been toying with the idea of doing *Titus* with Kick for some months so it didn't come as too much of a shock. You either have to want to do that particular play or you don't, and at least I knew I *almost* wanted to do it.

"Of course, I also wanted to work for the RSC, I desperately wanted to work for them. So it was a wonderful opportunity, and it was fortunate that I did have an interest in the play, but that didn't stop me from being terrified. There were moments when I thought it was a bad joke that I was actually there, in Stratford, doing it. I thought everyone would think, 'Here's this woman from the fringe who thinks she can do this play and it's a failure, so we'll kick her out again.'

"It's a horrendous play but the really exciting thing about it was that we did approach it blind. I had no easy solutions and I couldn't pretend that I had, so we worked as a group and talked and worked it through in rehearsal. It was a brilliant group with a brilliant Titus in Brian Cox and, through the way we worked, we did find astonishing things – that there was a really extraordinary black, comic aspect to it. I think that was the most remarkable discovery, and in making it, we found a way through it.

"There was a lot of input from the actors and I like that; it's how I work. Not only would I not be interested in working without input, I just wouldn't know how to. I think a director's role is to create the right environment and then step out of it for as long as possible and hope the actors will feel confident and brave enough to try to experiment. I can't see any other way of doing it."

From *Titus* she went to Bangladesh to direct a production of *The Tempest*. "In fact, it was the premiere of that play in Bangladesh and it was like nothing I've ever done before. It was an exciting, an enchanting time. What was interesting was that the area I was most frightened of, which was working in a different language, was not such a problem because we had very good translations and a good interpreter so that if you are working on a verse play under those conditions, you don't get lost. The problems lie elsewhere. You're dealing with actors from a different culture, unused to the rude honesty of the rehearsal room. I'm used to actors telling me what they think and if they really don't want to do something I need to know. Bengalis are always very polite and they didn't want to tell me if they didn't like something so that took some working out.

"Although we staged it in what is the most sophisticated and sought-after British Council auditorium in Dakkar, it was not as big as The Other Place, although it did have some lights. So, again, the production had to be simple and I also worked closely with the designer to ensure that it was of Bangladesh. It was a true challenge but not easy, because of the nature of the play. They had done other Shakespeare plays but all tragedies, and they see him as a tragic playwright – which is true in many ways – but they also see him as a great poet. They are a poetic race; Tagore was, after all, also a great poet. So they had to be persuaded that *The Tempest* was of interest to them, but they came round to it in the end."

So to the highly praised *King John*, its first production at Stratford since the mid-1970s. She did not choose that play, either. "Am I, I wonder, going to become the director who always does the little-known plays of Shakespeare? You know, next time *Timon of Athens* . . . But seriously, no, I didn't choose it, Adrian Noble asked me if I would like to do it. I was rather hoping I might be asked, although in another way I feared that I might." Adrian Noble has described it as a political play and one which directors are currently queueing up to undertake, but she has her own views about it.

She approached it, as she has all her Shakespearean productions, by a close and detailed examination of the text, always the text comes first. "I think that Shakespeare was actually experimenting when he wrote it and after doing so he changed how he worked. Although it's called *King John*, it's hard to see the king as the sole main character. There are *ten* major roles in the play and they share the major dialogue almost equally between them. So that in itself is a problem and then at least two of the scenes are tremendously long, they make up a quarter of the whole play, which must have been a real difficulty when you think that the audience had to stand in the days when the play was written. So it has very real technical problems."

Again, she has pared her cast to the bone although, as always, the text remains uncut. There is no set, her props consist of ladders and some chairs and the characters wear timeless garments which look as if they have been rummaged from the back of the wardrobe. The result is a fast production with a clear narrative.

"I agree with Adrian Noble that it is a political play, but its interest lies in what other things it is as well. Yes, it's about who this character called John actually is. He has no soliloquies, only the Bastard has soliloquies. It's about what his relationship with the Bastard is and why the play is called after him. These were the kind of things we had to try to find out, along with why it ends as it does when Hubert suddenly announces the arrival of the heir, Prince Henry. He's never even been mentioned before and by that time you are feeling that by far the most suitable person to be king is the Bastard.

"It's also a very funny play and I hope we got that across. It seems to depend to some extent on the audience on a particular night. If I was pushed, I would be tempted to say it was an Elizabethan black comedy about politics, perhaps an Elizabethan *Ubi Roi*, but I didn't set out with any of these ideas firmly fixed because that's not how I work. I could never arrive with a concept and then spend six weeks making damned sure it was never proved I was wrong. But I do now think that it is a black political comedy in which there are terrible casualties, the main ones being Arthur and Constance.

"You can't even say that John is a true villain. He's a man who makes some terrible decisions and the worst, when he decides to get rid of somebody, is one from which there is no going back. It's nothing like such a horrific play as *Titus* but when you are working on it there is something of the same feeling because you can feel quite at sea as it doesn't have any of the 'lines' through it that you expect and know you will get when, say, you are doing *Lear* or *The Tempest*.

With this play, you found yourself travelling down a certain path only to find yourself coming to a terrible stop. That is the difficulty.

"But I still applied the same principles for I feel if you do reach a dead-end then, as a director, it is your fault. It's no good thinking, oh well, it's an early play, not one of his best, it's not my fault. I happen to find it hard to believe that this particular author is ever at fault. The most exciting discoveries come in those moments when you have doubted and then you suddenly understand how it should be done. It can come when you wonder if you should cut the play but, as you work on it more and more, you realise exactly why those lines are there."

She has not cut it "not least because it has not been performed in the full version here for years, in fact I would argue it never has been played uncut. It's popular at the moment to cut the plays but I don't like to do so. I think there is a strong case for those plays which have been cut, or otherwise messed about, to be played as they were originally intended to be. It's because this has not happened that the myths have grown up that they are difficult or unactable or cannot be put across to today's audiences. If, say, in *Titus*, you've never had the chance as Marcus to play the whole speech to Lavinia, you'll never find out whether it's actable or not – in our case, it took us weeks to get it right but we found that it was, indeed, actable. That's what is so exciting about working on Shakespeare – it's believing that if you leave it to him, it will work. It's your own fault if it doesn't."

She finds it rewarding to follow a production through after it is running. "It is often forgotten that directors all have a different 'taste' for parts of the work. I like to stay with a production in its early weeks of performance, I think a director should. The press night is no more than the night the critics come. The RSC is unique in assuming a play will have a two-year life, which is very long, and as the actors are expected to come in enthusiastically night after night, it seems wrong that directors are not even expected to come in once a month, let alone once a week, if they don't want to."

She also feels that it is sad that a cast which has worked so hard to become an ensemble should then go off to do other things. "It would have been wonderful to go straight on and do something else with the same people, possibly workshop productions of *Timon*, say, or *Pericles*."

Offers have rained in on her. She would like to do the two parts of *Henry VI*, a *Hamlet* in the Swan. . . . She's been offered a production at the National Theatre and will almost certainly do it, and she will be directing Sophocles' *Electra* for the RSC in London.

Most of all, she wants to keep on directing Shakespeare but with decent intervals of rest between major productions. "I don't think I'd be any good at all if I just kept on doing one major production after the other – workshops would be different." One thing she is certain of: she intends to continue keeping it simple. "Actors are desperate to work properly on a great play. They are prepared to work on it uncut. They get tired of having it experimented with, cut about, having someone come along and put a 'concept' on it.

"That shouldn't be necessary. It shouldn't be difficult to be enthusiastic about Shakespeare, it's what so many of us want. It's there in Kick, and Cheek by Jowl and Shared Experience. The thought and driving force behind those companies and the RSC are, or should be, identical." Whether this is really so with regard to the RSC at the time of writing is a moot point. Meanwhile, Deborah Warner's way of doing Shakespeare, influenced by Brook and his empty space, is appealing to actors and audiences alike. Recently she was given what she describes as the "ultimate minimalist Shakespeare gift": the landlady of the Dirty Duck in Stratford gave her a two-inch-square edition of *King John*.

PHILIP HEDLEY

Born in Manchester, graduated from Sydney University, Australia. Founder student of E.15 Acting School. Artistic Director of Theatre Royal, Lincoln, and Midlands Arts Centre. Has directed plays in Sheffield, Stoke-on-Trent, Watford, Sydney, Vancouver and Khartoum and three musicals in West End. Joined Theatre Royal Stratford East as assistant to Joan Littlewood and Gerry Raffles, became chairman of board, appointed Artistic Director 1979. Has directed many new plays by writers such as Barrie Keeffe, Henry Livings, David Cregan and Alan Plater.

———————————

P hilip Hedley, Artistic Director of the Theatre Royal Stratford East in Newham, as it is now called, is variously described as a missionary, an idealist and a dangerous subversive, depending on one's point of view. The latter seems, on the surface, a total misnomer for such a mild-mannered man. Actors love working with him and scattered around the theatres of the country is a kind of Philip Hedley repertory company of actors who, when they are able to or when they can afford it, will troop off to E.15 to take part in a Hedley production.

Working in rehearsal he is endlessly patient and encouraging and appears to find no necessity to behave like a prima donna, although this is something which is rarer in the current generation of theatre directors than in the older one.

He grew up in Australia where he and his mother had

emigrated as a one-parent family. "I went to the cinema all the time, two or three times a week. I remember when I was about eight being asked to write an essay on what I wanted to be when I grew up and I wrote 'Stewart Granger' . . . Then I went to university where I did drama *all* the time and left really not knowing what to do next, whether to try to get a television training, or what."

It was then he came home from Australia to this country, "and went to a play at Stratford East – I don't know what prompted me to this day – and saw Ben Jonson's *Every Man In His Humour* and I was knocked sideways, I couldn't believe it. It is a great play but it was the way it was done that impressed me. I'd 'done' Ben Jonson at university and found it boring and seen boring productions but on this particular occasion I went down to Stratford East and arrived early so I had a coffee in the coffee bar.

"The girl serving was chatting to some locals who were in and I was fascinated, having grown up in Australia, to hear real cockneys and they were extremely funny and very witty. Then I walked into the theatre to see the play and there they were – the same kind of people, the same language, the same immediacy and I just couldn't believe it. I couldn't believe that anything could be that fresh or have such contact with the audience. I was in a daze afterwards and just walked up to someone who looked as if he might be in charge and said, 'What can I do here?'

"He looked pretty surprised because you don't do this – walk up and say, 'How can I devote my life to this place?' – but he suggested I attended the Saturday morning classes they were doing, which I did until they petered out. After that I did a six-month stint in weekly rep where the ASM before me had been Harold Pinter. That was at the Intimate Theatre at Palmers Green. After a time I thought, if this is what theatre's about, it's not a serious life for anyone. Four mornings' rehearsal was all you had for a play and then it went on. During the evenings you re-papered the walls of the set and that was the next week's design.

"Fortunately, at about this time I discovered that the E.15

Acting School had just got going and I managed to get a place although I started late. But I was a founder member of it. Littlewood had nothing to do with the school directly but lots of people who had worked with her did have. From there I went to Liverpool as an acting ASM, thinking that I wanted to be an actor, but I began doing work with young people on Saturday mornings and found I was putting far more into preparing work for them than into acting. I did some hard thinking and decided that the flotsam and jetsam of the actor's life was not what I wanted, I was far more attracted by directing. So I went back to E.15 and taught there for two years, directing plays all the time, which gave me experience. From there my first real director's job was at Lincoln Rep and within six months I was director of that theatre."

After Lincoln came the now defunct Midlands Arts Repertory Company, various other assignments and then back to E.15 and a rather difficult time working with Joan Littlewood. Even then there was a suggestion by Joan and Gerry Raffles that he should become co-director of the theatre, "but I wasn't ready for it", and after the death of Gerry Raffles there was a long gap when he did other things.

"By that time I'd been running companies one way or another for years, with all their many problems, on about two weeks' holiday a year and I was, you might say, written out. So there was no problem in turning down the job of Artistic Director when it was first offered to me. I never even got near to considering, 'Was it wise to take on *anything* which followed Joan Littlewood?' or questions like that."

Finally he agreed to run the theatre for three months "and one morning I was dashing to get ready and I thought, 'I want to do this, I really want to do this job more than anything else', and I now can't imagine doing anything else."

From that time on he worked on what he felt his vision of the Theatre Royal should be. "The list of shows we do is very eclectic. There are those we just don't do at all – I wouldn't do an Alan Ayckbourn or a very right-wing play (though you name me one single good right-wing playwright . . .). Alan Ayckbourn I like as a person and I admire his work a great deal but there's no point in our doing his plays because they are so widely performed everywhere else.

"What we do – and this is a very direct link with Joan – is work which tries to reflect the local community. I did, in fact, try to do this in Lincoln before I realised what a Joan kind of thing it was to do, but my feelings were strengthened by working with her here. At times we are accused cynically by people, who say, 'Oh, they're doing that Afro-Caribbean production because it will please Greater London Arts', and that annoys me deeply because these kinds of plays have been done here for thirty years. The whole idea is to have a link with the local community which then comes back to you – ideally by having writers coming through, like Barrie Keeffe and Tony Marchant. That's the most obvious example of it."

Nell Dunn's play *Steaming* is an example of what he means. "It was about the closure of a local Turkish baths and we used props from the real baths which were closing. It was based on a local story and it worked here as well as in the West End, but then she sent me some more plays which were not suitable as they dealt with the problems of a middle-class woman and they just wouldn't have worked here."

He is deeply interested in the question of marketing theatre and what is now happening in Thatcher's Britain. "A lot of reps are going for subscription seasons which, in my gut, I'm deeply against. That way you get the wrong audience for the wrong play and you can't be adventurous because you have to start pandering to your subscription people who are, by definition, middle-class. They've got diaries and can invest money in advance booking. People round our way won't book for tomorrow night, let alone every fourth Tuesday evening for nine months ahead. They aren't fools – they think we might not be there in six months' time and they won't get their money back.

"With every play I feel I'm starting all over again. We don't have a regular audience in the general sense. We have regular Afro-Caribbean or young audiences who come for specific kinds of play and family audiences who always come to the pantomime but their turn may not come round again for a year although some do start to come to see other things. However, in marketing terms we're doing exactly what the experts tell you never to do. They say you should stick with one thing, as Greenwich has: they aim at the white middle-class audience which lives in one end of their borough. You never see a black face at Greenwich."

His plays have caused rampant fury in some quarters, especially among Conservative backbenchers in the House of Commons who blew their collective top when he put on Howard Brenton's *A Short Sharp Shock*. This has made ordinary funding difficult enough, let alone getting the commercial sponsorship, the "Enterprise Culture" so beloved of the current Arts Minister, Richard Luce, and the present Arts Council.

A play by Barrie Keeffe featured a strip by a Mrs Thatcher look-alike who discarded a garment with the announcement of each new cut in education or the NHS, and this also provoked questions in the House. "When our fund raiser tentatively approached the local Midland Bank for possible funds he was shown the door with the words, 'No, you do plays against Mrs Thatcher'." The only organisation to show any interest in their performance of *A Short Sharp Shock* "was MI5, a representative of which, thinly disguised as an expert on the Labour Party, came to my flat to advise on a discussion of the text with two of our board members."

The title of a play performed in the 1987 season, *Pork Pies* by Vince Foxall, might on the surface, he says, have looked attractive to manufacturers of cooked meats but would have got nowhere when they discovered it was rhyming slang for "lies" and was based on the true story of a detective who made allegations about the way his colleagues fiddled the figures to show a higher rate of solving crimes. "Again, the only firm that showed interest in that was a firm of solicitors acting for the Police Federation."

He is not impressed with the examples he is asked to follow and cites the RSC. "Its chairman tells us their Royal Insurance Company deal 'will be greeted with delight and gratitude, not just by the RSC but by the art world generally,' but is it *really* worth the RSC changing its logo to make the word 'insurance' bigger than 'Shakespeare'? Especially when it is only benefiting by what I estimate to be about two and a half per cent of its turnover in the next three years."

When he planned a Shakespeare production, with a rehearsal period which included an educational programme in local schools, "We pulled out all the stops. We contacted any friends of influence. But even this worthy combination, Shakespeare, education, a poor district and letters signed by two knights of the realm, produced nothing. We've given up the serious search for sponsorship for shows now. It hasn't proved worth the considerable investment of time, imagination, money and the loss of a degree of self-respect we've had to put up with."

This is at extreme odds with a letter from Alexander Jules which appeared in *The Guardian* on 18 September 1987 in reply to an article on this subject by Hedley. The writer finds himself unable to sympathise with Hedley's dilemma, suggesting that he is "unaware of the present financial climate within the Arts" and speaking out robustly for commercial sponsorship which can be found "if the right product is available and while we may have to lower our standards in this respect, this is the only way now to make ends meet".

Yet it is partly the difficulties which keep Philip Hedley at Stratford East, that, "and the fact that I have a marvellous board who really *don't* interfere in the choice of play. I don't consult them about what play I'm going to do, I tell them. If by chance there isn't a board meeting at the right time but I'm able to get a brochure out about the next few productions, then I might well announce what I'm going to do to the press before I let the board know – though very often I can't get a brochure out because I can't plan that far ahead. Mind you, that's not always a bad thing because if you aren't careful you can find yourself with 'brochure theatre', as well as subscription theatre, and putting on plays and using actors and directors just because you had to put something in the brochure, not because they are the best choice. My board treat me in the way I believe one should treat guest directors: once you have made the decision then you have to let them get on and possibly make their own mistakes, and you have to support them in both the good things and the bad things they do."

This freedom from his board means that Hedley himself been much exercised over Clause 29 of the Local Government Act, the woolly edict which makes it illegal for a local authority or other public body actively to "promote" homo-sexuality – whatever that might mean. He feels this must be tested.

"Of course, I wouldn't do a play if I didn't think it was a good play and passed all the usual tests from its plot to whether or not the season has been sufficiently balanced in its content, but then I happened to notice an article in *The Guardian* about a play by Lorca called *The Public* which had just been done in Paris and which had naturally been banned during Franco's time, although it has been performed in Spain since. It's a kind of dream play of highly theatrical images – death, art, censorship, love and sex, all threaded together – in which the author's homosexuality is released in the way, for example, E. M. Forster's was in *Maurice*."

In this case he would be looking for a wider audience – regular theatregoers, students, teachers, homosexuals, liberal-minded folk, "and it might seem an unusual choice for Stratford East, but remember Joan Littlewood was a champion of Lorca long before he was fashionable or even known much in British theatre. A good many people from this borough did, however, turn up on the Clause 29 march so I believe there is a community for it here, although obviously I would also have to go for the London-wide audience as well." He doesn't see it as being the same thing as putting on an indifferent piece for the sake of being provocative or as agitprop, but as a poetic and creative piece of theatre which is highly defensible artistically.

When we spoke he was hoping to do the play and expected the enthusiastic support of his board, "although if anyone gets sued under this act it will be the local authority, not the theatre. I don't mean that makes me feel safe because we would obviously suffer heavily too and I've already had an off-the-record warning that if anything is done on the homosexual front it could make future grants difficult. This particular man was speaking to me in a very elegant room with a tall window behind him and the combination of that elegance and this quiet voice talking about 'my own good' gave me a real whiff of Nazi Germany in the thirties. I had two people with me and I was so stunned at what he was saying I asked him to repeat it and he actually said it twice . . ."

Returning again to the stoutness of his board, he recalled that when the Police Federation was threatening action if he went ahead and put on *Pork Pies*, the story made the front pages of all the papers, "which was marvellous publicity. Only afterwards did I realise that I'd never felt the need to ring anyone on the board to reassure them about the play and that everything would be all right, nor had the chairman or anyone else from the board phoned me. They regarded it as a natural part of my job to be controversial.

"So we go from that controversial end of the scale to the absolutely conventional family entertainment, like melodrama and pantomime and Sunday night variety shows. I don't think I'm boasting when I say I can't think of another theatre which does our *range* of work. That, and the close involvement with the community suits me, it suits my working-class origins.

"Years ago I was in New York at the Metropolitan Opera and as I looked out of the windows I realised there really were noses pressed up against the glass, drug addicts, down-and-outs, standing just the other side of the plate glass from the people in furs and you thought, what's going on? How can you allow this to happen and not be on the front line?"

He is hooked on the constant battle and all the problems he faces, "but if it turned secure I'd leave. I love insecurity – real security would be death of the soul to me."

ROGER REDFARN

Born in London, trained for the theatre in Birmingham. Worked extensively in regional rep. Was assistant to the Director of the Welsh Theatre Company, followed by five years as Associate Director of the Belgrade Theatre, Coventry. Worked as a freelance director all over the world. His first West End production was a revival of *The King and I*. His credits include *The School for Scandal* by Richard Brinsley Sheridan, *Juno and the Paycock* and *Shadow of a Gunman* by Sean O'Casey and the musicals *West Side Story*, *The Sound of Music, South Pacific*. Became Artistic Director of the Theatre Royal, Plymouth, in 1984.

Artistic director of one of the largest and most successful regional producing theatres, the Theatre Royal in Plymouth, Roger Redfarn is also nationally and internationally known as a director of musicals.

He was brought up in Cambridge, the eldest of six, and certainly without a theatrical background. "I used to go to just about everything that came to Cambridge – variety, music hall, straight plays, everything, although I particularly loved ballet and dance. I remember the occasion when we were all having a family meal and my father asked me what I thought I wanted to do when I left school and I told him I wanted to go into the theatre. The whole family was stunned and my father's reaction was to tell me to go off and clean my bicycle and I remember the tears dropping down on to it as I did it.

"However, on leaving school I did agree to do a catering course as my parents were so concerned that I should have what they thought of as a 'proper job', but my heart wasn't in it. One day, I saw an advertisement for the Birmingham School of Speech and Drama and I was determined to go. I went along to the local committee that gave grants and asked if I could have a grant to study there. A lady asked me what I thought I could live on and I said five pounds and she said however did I think I would eat, and I told her I could live on brown bread and baked beans – it shows how unrealistic I was. But I did get a grant and I did go to Birmingham."

He helped keep himself in Birmingham by working in a variety of capacities at both the Birmingham Rep and Alexandra theatres until he had finished his course, "when I had some more luck". The luck was an offer of a job as assistant stage manager at the Lincoln Rep on seven pounds a week, working both in the theatre and touring around the countryside. This was followed by Scottish Opera ("as general dogsbody"), before a meeting with the theatre director, Warren Jenkins, sent them both off to Wales to found a Welsh National Theatre.

They set up home in a disused nunnery – "it became disused but nuns were still living in it when we took it over. To found the new company Warren had had a brief-case and a cheque – nothing else. We used the nunnery as our headquarters and for workshops and we toured all over Wales, but we never did get a theatre. It was while I was with Warren in Wales that I started to direct. The first production was John Barton's *The Hollow Crown* and I also did *The Caretaker* by Harold Pinter and *The Rivals* by Richard Brinsley Sheridan. But after five years with still no sign of a building we'd both had enough and when Warren had the chance to take over the Belgrade Theatre in Coventry he took it and I went with him."

Coventry was a baptism of fire. "I did fifty-two main house productions in five years, ranging from Shakespeare to Ray

Cooney via Ben Jonson, John Arden and O'Casey. I learned how to direct simply by doing it. Actually, I don't believe there is any other way – there's too much academic hoo-ha going on in the theatre nowadays. So I had that long period at Coventry and towards the end of it, when things were going well, I did two or three big musicals. Then articles began to appear in papers like *The Stage* and, indeed, national newspapers, saying how I'd revived the big musical and become a kind of king of the musicals. It came from nowhere and then the Arts Council asked us if we would tour a large-scale American musical – this was back in 1973 before Cameron Mackintosh started to do it.

"Along they came and saw the Belgrade's *West Side Story* and asked if we would tour that. We didn't know what to say – we didn't have the facilities or the expertise or the people – but, anyway, we agreed and did *The Pajama Game*. It was a case of touring Glyndebourne opera, the Festival Ballet and the Belgrade Theatre Coventry with *The Pajama Game*. A number of people saw it and I began to get offers to do commercial things. I knew nothing about the commercial side – I was in awe of London and the West End. I never even considered I might work there.

"I was asked to do a production of *The King and I* which I did for a tour. Harold Fielding saw it and it went into London in 1976. I couldn't believe that I had been put up for a Winston Churchill award by people who had come to see my work at Coventry. It was given me to go to America for three months and study the American musical and while I was there, quite by chance I met Harold Fielding who said, 'We've been looking for you. You'd better get back to England as we're taking your production of *The King and I* into town.' There was a terrific to-do about it – even editorials in the papers – and I still don't know why. The *Evening Standard* carried a big piece about me saying, 'This man will never be out of the West End' – after which I think it was about three years before I was asked to do anything there again."

When I first spoke to him he was rehearsing the musical

South Pacific which was also to go into the West End. How does he start work on a musical?

"Well, to some extent it depends on the musical. Most of those I've done since I've been in Plymouth have been proven. The *Olivers*, the *Sound of Musics*, the *South Pacifics*, they're established and they work. But you have to have a respect for each one before you start. The problem with *South Pacific*, which had not been done in a big way for thirty-eight years, was to respect what was there before but also make it relevant to 1987. What has pleased me about it is that nobody has said it is old-fashioned or dusty. So you have to treat the shows as if they were written yesterday and how do you start?

"One of the basic things you have to know when you embark on a big musical is how much money you have to spend. I knew *South Pacific* would only work if it sounded wonderful, so I had twenty-seven in the orchestra and a cast of thirty-nine. We were only able to do it because we knew we had commercial backing and that it would go into town. So the aim is to make it sound marvellous – that's terribly important.

"I have a tremendous respect for Rodgers and Hammerstein, I think they were masters of their craft. So my approach was to treat *South Pacific* as if it had just been written and was quite new. We used a great deal of modern technology: there are travalators and big metal doors, waterfalls – it's quite spectacular. I did not base anything on the original London version because I never saw it.

"It's a show which has more to it than might immediately appear. People talk about Rodgers and Hammerstein as being sugary and romantic but this is a show about sex, racial tolerance and intolerance and about one culture being totally destroyed by another. That's what happened. There was this wonderful Pacific culture which was destroyed by invaders who came in and smashed their way of life and I found all that very interesting indeed. It's also about war and is a good anti-war piece and I think today you can make a lot more of those things than you could when it was first written.

"In fact, when they transferred the show from the stage to

the screen one of the best numbers in it, 'You've got to be carefully taught', which is about how we are born equal and you have to be taught to hate people whose eyes are a different shape or whose skin is a different colour, did not go into the film. They just did not allow it to go into it because it spelled out that you had actually to be taught racial prejudice.

"The other main point to make about directing a musical is that it does require an enormous amount of organisation. There's so much that you have to bring together – music, orchestra, chorus, principals, design, lighting, sound – but all on a big scale and that has to be done well in advance. In a way, it's no different from a play; it's just more complicated. You also have to think about singing ability as well as acting talent and which is the more important really depends on the show. *South Pacific* has to be well acted *and* well sung and Gemma Craven, Bertice Reading and Emile Belcourt were my first and only three choices and I got them all. Casting a musical is always difficult but this was particularly so and I really wouldn't have been happy with anyone else.

"It's a question of weighing up and considering the values of different musicals. For instance, *Oliver* isn't so musically demanding so I could cast a good actor, Derek Griffiths, as Fagin. I didn't have to look for a singing voice first.

"Nowadays it is not unusual for a musical not to have a conventional chorus but *South Pacific* was the first one which was written without one. Rodgers and Hammerstein were amazing innovators – there's no chorus and everyone has a name. They all play parts and this was unheard of when it was written. There was no choreography in the show because there were no dancers and I wasn't allowed to add them so I choreographed it, so far as any was needed, along with an assistant. As soon as you go into dance you go into an unreal situation and there are no unreal situations in that show. All the big songs, like 'Nothing Like a Dame', had, therefore, to be staged like a scene in a pageant or an epic play because these men were frustrated animals – we talked about it in those terms, not in terms of 'you put your left foot behind your right and then do a twist' or any of that kind of thing.

"We forget now how remarkable those immediately post-war musicals were. In *Oklahoma* the curtain went up on an empty stage with just one woman churning some butter. The first night audience didn't know what to do: they couldn't understand it. There was a sensation when news leaked out during the rehearsals for the first production of *The King and I* that the King, the star of the show, actually *died* at the end: it was unheard of. There would be no Andrew Lloyd Webber or Sondheim without Rodgers and Hammerstein. Sondheim was their protégé; he actually went to them as a boy of twelve with a script for a musical."

Like all artistic directors of regional theatres, Roger Redfarn's work divides into two: he is not only responsible for individual productions but for the artistic policy of the theatre as a whole and for selecting what goes on. After a number of increasingly successful years in the commercial theatre in this country and abroad, he came to Plymouth because he eventually reached the stage when he felt he had had enough. "I felt that I wanted to go back to a regional theatre. Coventry had been wonderful. Of course, there was never as much money as one would have liked but there was enough for me to do what I wanted to do to a reasonable standard.

"I realised the kind of job I wanted would be really difficult to find and I also wanted it to be a challenge. I didn't want to go into comfy three-weekly rep." He knew about the Theatre Royal, had visited it and also knew it had severe problems – "nobody's fault, any new child has teething troubles. It had been built as a great act of faith without those who built it having any opportunity of thinking of its future, and quite by chance they were looking for an Artistic Director." He also recognised that at that stage the theatre had no policy except that the need was felt for a regional theatre, not just a touring house.

The theatre board was planning to appoint a General Manager as well as an Artistic Director "which meant they must in future want a mixed programme with an opportunity to explore. It also meant they wanted something more than three-weekly rep., which wouldn't have worked anyway for the main house has an epic stage, it's a lyric house.

"The interview was *bizarre*. I thought the competition would be enormous. I don't mean that I expected to find Trevor Nunn down there, but I thought there would be the cream of the cream. In a way, I was a bit worried that there wasn't. I wondered why everybody was staying away! I had the first interview, then there was another and we all had lunch during which a man came up to me and said, 'Oh, you're still here!' 'Yes,' I said, 'should I go?' and he replied, 'Oh yes, don't hang about . . .' I'd wanted to see a show that night and I had assumed that at the end of the afternoon we'd be told who'd got the job but the man said, 'No, no, we can't do that – we don't even know if we're going to get an Arts Council grant yet!' So off I went.

"I knew that Andrew Welch, who was to be General Manager, had come over from Hong Kong for the interview virtually for the day, and I thought that was even odder. Whoever was supposed to become Artistic Director surely needed to talk to him in case he said, 'Well, actually, we're going to do nothing but opera and ballet but once a year we'll let you do a play.' Anyway, I stayed the night and in the small hours of the morning Andrew rang me from Heathrow where he was catching a plane for Hong Kong and said if they got a grant and I was offered the job, would I take it? He was sure that together we could come up with a policy. Finally, at the end of the week when they knew they had got a grant, they rang me up and offered me the job.

"When I arrived the whole building was very tense. There was no sense of direction and everything was in a bad way so I kept a very low profile for a month – almost pretended I wasn't in the building just so I had an idea of what was going on. People kept asking me what we were going to do and at that stage I just didn't know.

"The first thing I realised was that we had no money to do shows. We had enough to staff the building but that was all. The only way we could do a show was in conjunction with a commercial management and that's how it started – out of total necessity. The first two years were really hard, sleepless night after sleepless night: finances, relationships, getting it right. Then people started coming with wonderful propositions for Plymouth. I did Kenneth Graham's *Wind in the Willows* with an all-star cast and packed the building and the board realised that if we did shows people wanted to see they would come.

"First of all I had to get the main house right, studio and young people's theatre had to come second. I did do a Drum [studio] season which went well, so I knew it could work, although we had no money for it." A big traditional panto with Danny La Rue followed, "to give them glamour and for people who never usually go to the theatre; to hit them visually and give them Danny's warmth was more important than anything. They flocked in and somehow you felt the building wanting to turn the corner.

"I went on from there to do things I thought people would enjoy because the most vital thing was that they should come into the building and then see what they wanted to see. There were some who thought it was a white elephant, some who thought it was élitist, some who were frightened to come inside because they weren't wearing nice enough clothes. We had to break down all those barriers and say, 'I don't care what you're wearing, come on in! It's *your* building, *your* rates are paying for it', and slowly they began to be quite proud of us. The real turning point was *The Sound of Music*. We had a small tour lined up and then something went wrong and the commercial management suddenly decided not to back it. If we went ahead we knew we stood the chance of losing thousands of pounds and, in the case of Andrew and me, of losing our jobs.

"We talked it over with the board who said that everything we had done so far had worked and what did I think? I told them it was the biggest box office musical in history and I thought we could make it work. So we did it with our fingers crossed, but we couldn't cast Maria. So I thought, there's nothing for it – I'll make a star in Plymouth! I held open auditions and saw two hundred and eighty girls and couldn't find one. I was sweating. Then the two hundredth and eighty-first girl walked on and she was so perfect. She was from Cork. I got her an Equity card and she did her first professional show. At the end of the first night the audience stood and cheered. They made her a star – Plymouth had done it, not me. She's back now playing the lead in our *Brigadoon*. It was very important to the city.

"Now the theatre is properly part of the life of the city. It's accepted. The day I arrived here to work the taxi driver who brought me to the theatre told me, 'I shouldn't work there. Nobody goes', and there was a cartoon on the front of the local paper showing a man, his wife and two children leaving the theatre and the little boy is saying, 'Dad, I didn't see the white elephant . . .'"

Now the theatre runs seven days a week. There is a flourishing studio theatre, Sunday concerts and variety, week-end workshops, shows do local and national tours, during the summer they branched into open air theatre in the grounds of Mount Edgcumbe House. Commercial managements are encouraged to a degree, "but carefully . . . we don't want to get into a situation where we totally rely on them. We're underfunded by the Arts Council for historical reasons – about £500,000 a year less than is given to Sheffield, Leicester or Birmingham – but hopefully things will get better. The money from the 'Glory of the Garden' [Arts Council report] does allow us to keep the programme going in the studio, although there are still insufficient funds for actors, designers and musicians in the main house. This means we either put on inexpensive productions we can fund ourselves or we turn to the commercial managements for shows like our musicals and when these leave Plymouth we get a royalty for the show."

The policy enables the theatre to employ over two hundred people full time and give them security, although he recognises that commercial backers would not support the classic plays he'd like to do. Michael Bogdanov's company, however, did start the *Henry* plays in Plymouth.

Above all else, he sees his role of Artistic Director as

a comprehensive one, and that includes ensuring a good atmosphere for those working in the theatre. "I like to be in constant touch with everyone from the wardrobe to the restaurant. I think – and hope – I'm a good company director. I can sense when there is something wrong or when someone is unhappy. I sympathise with the problems of actors and get on well with them. Of course, there will always be some who are difficult, although when you look at the really great ones – the Gielguds, the Oliviers, the Jacobis – they never are. Look at Judi Dench! She's one of the greatest actresses we've ever had and you couldn't find a nicer person or someone who is easier to work with. I worship her. I sincerely hope I am good at company spirit because that is essential.

"It's been a hard slog and it will never get easy and we have to keep on improving it, but what has been marvellous for Andrew and me is that people, including members of the City Council, have come up to us and said, 'I was dead against this building – now I'm all for it'."

JUDI DENCH

One of our best-known and best-loved actresses. Worked at the Old Vic, Nottingham Playhouse, Royal Shakespeare Company, the National Theatre, extensively in the West End and on television and to a lesser extent in films. Has won numerous awards. Created Dame of the Order of the British Empire 1988. Famous roles include: Beatrice, Titania, Viola, Isabella, Hermione/Perdita, Imogen, title part in *Mother Courage* by Bertolt Brecht, Juno in *Juno and the Paycock* by Sean O'Casey, Portia, Cleopatra, etc.

A memorable Beatrice herself in the 1976 John Barton production of *Much Ado About Nothing*, which he set at the height of the Raj in nineteenth-century India, it is not, perhaps, surprising that when Kenneth Branagh decided to set up his Renaissance Theatre Company that he should invite Judi Dench to direct the play for him. With her long experience of playing Shakespeare, had the task daunted her at all, did she find such a new experience frightening?

"By the time I got to the first preview I was terrified, absolutely hysterical. I rang up Michael [her husband, the actor Michael Williams] and he was so concerned he said he'd drop everything and be down in the morning. I told him they didn't laugh – they didn't even know when the interval was. I felt as if I was in a pile-up of fifteen coaches on the M1. Then that night I made a lot of lists, took a sleeping pill and went to sleep and rang him the next day and said, 'It's all right, I can manage, you don't need to come down'; and the next night was just marvellous."

The critics gave her rave reviews – "clear", "Shakespeare new-minted", "delightful", "magical" were just some of the adjectives used.

She began, she says, conventionally enough by blocking the play, working out the moves. "Perhaps if I had far more experience it might be possible to manage without this and do it as I go along, like Peter Brook, but I felt this was the way for me, to get some kind of a framework. I also felt the actors needed a frame within which they could work as well.

"I didn't enjoy that part too much or even the first reading. I also found, on the first day, that I couldn't stop talking about tight white trousers! I got onto the subject and couldn't stop it, so I was sent up from the beginning. The trousers were all part of how I saw the design."

All who saw the production agreed that the text came across with crystal clarity. Had she worked hard with them on it before formal rehearsals began? "No. I worked on it as we went along. I told them we must obey the text, we must look at the lines and the half-lines and the caesuras, and it must be well spoken. As Peter [Peter Hall] said when we were rehearsing *Antony and Cleopatra* at the National, only by doing that will you make sense of it and learn to breathe in the right place. He is very worried about how young actors speak Shakespeare now so I thought it would be a good thing to pass the message on. So I was on at them about that.

"I was really very glad as so many of the notices said it was very clearly and intelligently spoken: that was such a relief. Although I'd been happy to say I'd direct it when I was first asked over a year before, as the actual date drew nearer I had those mounting nightmares, thinking it was like someone saying to me, 'You *are* going to dance *Les Sylphides*?' or, 'Would you like to do some brain surgery, a little trepanning, perhaps?' It was like that.

"My way of tackling it was to make masses of lists, just masses of lists. I also sat down and really read the play because

I realised that all I knew thoroughly was Beatrice's bit. I made lists of who appears when, of how and why and of who could double. You see Derek [Jacobi], Gerry [Geraldine McEwan] and I had to cast fifteen actors who could do all three plays [*Much Ado*, *Hamlet* and *As You Like It*]. That was horrific! It was so *difficult*. There's plenty of talent but I had to think, will these people get on, will they be able to double? Then you found the one who said, 'I don't want to do that', and you feel mortally hurt and take it as a slight to yourself, or they say, 'I'll do it if I can play that and that', so the juggling around and shennanigans was amazing. In time it came together."

The production was simple and straightforward and, unlike the much-criticised 1988 Royal Shakespeare Company production of the same play which opened about the same time, without gimmickry or a plethora of technical effects. "There couldn't be: a) there wasn't any money and I think one of the most attractive things of being asked to direct a play is coming in *under* budget, and b) we were in the Birmingham Rep studio so there were very few facilities and we had to do it in such a way that we could turn the show round after a matinée and do one play in the afternoon and another in the evening, so that was imposed on us really through expediency.

"As to design, I think someone, Charles Osborne possibly, said I'd obviously thought the sight of young men in tights was too distracting! That made me laugh so much. Actually, I felt that if you have people coming on in tights, what people nowadays think of as fancy dress be it Elizabethan or anything else, they not only think that the costume is quite foreign to them but also that the text will be foreign to them too. That's why I did go on about the trousers. I thought we'd set it in the period where men, for the first time, did wear trousers and, anyway, the play seemed to fit in very well with the Napoleonic wars and Italy. I wanted it to be a world with which people could readily identify.

"I think it did work well. I found that all my training in history of art and wanting to be a designer (and not an actress in those days) came to the fore tremendously because I saw everything in a series of pictures. That seemed to me to be very important because I would think, oh, I know why I did that! There's a point where an actress is leaning over something and there's a marvellous Goya of a girl leaning just like that. Also James Villiers comes in and leans down and there's a wonderful portrait of an Elizabethan gentleman which looks very like him, while the girls in their white dresses were very Degas and Impressionist."

There were, for this writer at least, strong overtones of Judi Dench's own Beatrice in the performance of the young Samantha Bond. "So I've been told. No, I never ever said to her, 'You should say it this way or that way.' I did say things like, 'I think you should look again at that sentence because I think it can say more things than you are intending.' I'm so delighted because very often when I played it I would get a laugh on 'Kill Claudio!' and they don't get a laugh, which is entirely due to their facility and their talent. I just kept on emphasising that it was more important to tell the story than to turn it into a great comedy which gets belters all the time. I'm not interested in that.

"I told them about Ronnie Eyre who, after the first run-through of Dion Boucicault's *London Assurance* when we'd all laughed and laughed and absolutely sailed through it and thought we were going to do the most wonderful show, said to us, 'I've had a splendid morning and I wouldn't exchange it for anything but you can't do it that way because the story is completely muddied in favour of huge laughs for all sorts of reasons.' It's a good lesson to learn. Painful, when you think you've got up something rather well, but nevertheless a good lesson."

Some years ago when we had discussed the play she had told me how strongly she felt that Beatrice had been badly betrayed by Benedict earlier, before the play begins, and that was how she had played it. It was the way Samantha Bond played it too. "It really is just said in the play. She says of her heart, 'once before he won it of me with false dice, therefore your grace may well say I have lost it': it's quite clear. It's not always played that way but there's no doubt about it.

The decision is whether you want to pick up on it or just gloss over it. Samantha felt it too.

"We tried to analyse what every single thing meant and if we couldn't come to a conclusion over something then we just decided to say it with confidence! Michael Benthall used to tell me that so long as you said something with confidence you could get by."

Did she ever have to get tough with them? "Bossy? School-marmish? Yes, I did, because what happened was that after I'd tried to iron out all those extraordinary stresses that we all do in the text then you get a lot of false stresses. I know I do it and I could see it in them, so that was what I had to keep on about. You often do that when the play is not going well and you try to push it on with false stresses. But we did have some huge laughs and they did corpse a lot during the first run-through and I, normally the leader of the corpsers, had to sit there absolutely stony-faced. I could see it was very funny but I thought, how on earth are we going to get through it? In the end I just said, 'Cut it' and we went on. But I was quite tough about things I felt instinctively were right.

"Although I loved people coming with ideas at the beginning, you have to separate yourself off in the end. The buck stops with you and you have to say, 'Please, I don't want you to do that again.' Then you creep in on them and go to a performance and there they are doing it . . . and you go round afterwards like a tornado. I found on tour, too, when I went and took masses of notes that they didn't want them at the end as they were all rushing off to catch trains to London to go home, and they didn't want to come in early, either. So I became paranoid about that and thought they'd all had a meeting and decided they would do that to me, but both Derek and Gerry said it happened to them too."

Working with Kenneth Branagh was, she says, "hugely enjoyable. He's very receptive and, indeed, frightened although he gives the impression of being terribly confident. But he's not that confident. He often doesn't trust himself. The production has really jelled now. It's very, very sharp, gentle but sharp. And Kenneth is having a ball with it. He acts on a razor edge. I told him, 'My God, your courage is amazing because you dare to do things I certainly wouldn't.' In the soliloquies he gets belters because he now trusts himself. He used to do a lot of looking down and it used to drive me mad so I told him that thing Jack Minster used to say, 'It's no good looking on the floor, dear boy, all you'll find there is the play!' They all used to do it a lot.''

How did she cope with the director's nightmare – the technical rehearsal? "Actually, I loved it. The bit I liked best was sound levels and lighting it. I thought, this is it, it's *son et lumière* so I'll forget the actors. I really adored it. I did it in five hours. I was lucky because I had Brian Harris to light it, which was very good, and Jenny Tirimani, the designer, was excellent as well, so I had a great crew. Possibly, therefore, I had it very lightly and easily.''

Did she feel a sense of loss once the show had actually gone on? "Yes, I did. And I couldn't bear to feel they were going on to rehearse *Hamlet* and *As You Like It*, because they were not mine any more. There is always that moment when the audience comes in and the baby learns to manage completely without you. You can smack it every now and then but it just laughs right in your face and keeps on doing it. It's gone from you entirely and you no longer have any connection with it, except that your name's on the programme.''

Will she do it again? "I don't know. I've honestly no idea. People seem to think that once you've directed a play you'll want to do it again and again but at the moment I doubt that I'll ever do it again.''

DEREK JACOBI

One of our best-known classical actors. Began his career at Birmingham Rep, then went to the National Theatre, Prospect Theatre Company, Royal Shakespeare Company. Has played most of the major classic Shakespearean roles both on stage and television. Also title roles in *Peer Gynt* by Henrik Ibsen and *Cyrano de Bergerac* by Edmond Rostand. Television includes Claudius in *I, Claudius*, by Robert Graves, Richard II, Hamlet and Philby. Films include *The Day of the Jackal*, *The Hunchback of Notre Dame*, *Inside the Third Reich*, *The Human Factor* and *Little Dorrit*. He has won numerous Best Actor awards.

The Renaissance Theatre Company offered Derek Jacobi the chance to direct for the first time, following on from Judi Dench and Geraldine McEwan. He could hardly have had a greater test for his play was *Hamlet*.

Did he choose his play? "Oh, no. It chose me. The story behind it is that Ken [Kenneth Branagh] at the age of sixteen was deciding what to do with his life. He wanted to be a journalist, in fact, and was already writing book reviews and that sort of thing for the local paper, when he went over to Oxford one night to see a production of *Hamlet* – that was my first one with the Prospect Theatre Company. He then decided that he wanted to be an actor; that was going to be his life. Two years later, when I was doing *Hamlet* for the second time for Prospect, at the Old Vic, I had a letter from

Ken, asking if he could come to see me to talk about acting in general and *Hamlet* in particular.

"I wrote back and said I'd be delighted to see him – I didn't actually know it was Ken, of course – and he came along at all of eighteen and we talked about acting and he said that one day he wanted to play Hamlet and I wished him luck, etc. Years later I got to hear of Kenneth Branagh and thought, that's the boy who asked me for an interview.

"Later still I met him and got to know him, and when he had the idea of Renaissance doing three plays directed by actors it seemed to him the most natural thing that the actor to do his *Hamlet* should be the actor he first saw play it. So he asked me and my first reaction was, no, I'm an actor not a director, but the second was, I'll probably never play it again myself so the next best thing is to direct it. We chatted and he thought there'd be no problem. So I said, 'OK, let's have a go.'

"That's when the problems started! I had to go to America in Hugh Whitemore's *Breaking the Code*, and would only arrive back just before the play went into rehearsal. I was in the United States for eight months so I had to plan everything at one remove. The company was cast and brought together and I was kept informed of who had been engaged – some I knew and some I didn't – and then Ken and the designer and Kenneth Parker, from the company, came over to New York for a week and that was when we started really working on it. I needed them to tell me who in the company could play what; I knew who could play the big roles but what about the Bernardos and Marcelluses? So it was really all cast before I'd met fifty per cent of them. As it happened, it worked out marvellously well."

Was it strange to go back to that text having played the part himself? "Yes, it was. I didn't intend using the full text, I wanted to cut it but I wanted it to be my own version of the play, my own cuts. While I was in New York I spent a lot of time cutting it, transposing a couple of scenes and some speeches and, in a couple of instances, parcelling out between two people dialogue which normally would have been said by one person. For instance, I wanted to lay more emphasis on Gertrude and Ophelia. There was nothing textually that I could do for Ophelia, but you do see her around much more in the production. You see more of her, for instance, between the play scene and the mad scene so that, hopefully, you have some indication of what's happened to her.

"With Gertrude I could actually give her some extra dialogue. Claudius' long speech welcoming Rosencrantz and Guildenstern, for example, is now spoken between him and Gertrude, not so that they finish one another's sentences but so that he says some of it and so does she. I wanted her more vocally involved in the scene than is usually the case. One hopes that any imaginative leaps in the production of the play will be textual — not scenic, not costumes, or props, or anything like that; that all the newness of this interpretation comes through the text. Any new meanings should come from that text, from well-worn phrases, that's what we're aiming for whether we succeed or not. It's all, *all* from the text.

"The thrust of the narrative, the story in the play, is so marvellous. The text and the narrative are the linchpins of what I tried to do. The play's the thing. Hopefully it gives the play back to the actors and lets them use their own imaginations on the play and on the text, rather than bind them into a straitjacket of some kind."

A production of *Much Ado* with a MASH-type army and oppressive costumes, had recently opened at Stratford to universal dislike. Does he feel that actors in some Shakespeare productions have been swamped by both the director's concept and the design? "I think it is very difficult for the major companies. They have to plan the sets and costumes so far ahead because they're doing so many plays, but what, in fact, that says to the actors is, 'There's the set, there's the costumes, there's the picture you have to make — make it!' You can end up half way through rehearsals saying, 'I don't want to do this or wear that', and the response is that you have to because of the look of the picture they want to create. All too often that picture is against what the actor is feeling inside.

"I wanted the design for *Hamlet* to be very simple. I worried a lot initially about the concept and as I was working with Clifford Williams at the time, I went to him and said, 'Clifford, what do directors *do*?' 'Well,' he said, 'basically all you have to do is direct the traffic – get them on and off and make sure they don't knock into each other!' I could understand that but what about the *concept*, the great director's mind like a searchlight on the play . . . turning the play *bouleversé* and all that sort of thing? Then I realised that what I had to give to this particular play was a knowledge of it in performance.

"I did it twice on stage and once on TV. I played it on proscenium stages, round stages, indoor stages, outdoor stages, stages in China, Japan, Egypt, whatever, an enormous backlog of experience of the play in performance. That, I felt, was a quality particularly unique to me in directing this play, so why not use it? That's what I've got to give it.

"It was that word 'performance' that stuck and of all the plays it is the one which is most about playing. The play is about acting, it even has a company of actors in it who do a play; people are acting, are pretending, none of them are what they seem, they're all giving a performance. So then I thought – not as a concept but just as a setting – let it look like a theatre. What should that look like? Very simple: it needs curtains, red curtains like tabs, and basically that's what it is. When people come in it looks like a straightforward theatre.

"So the whole play is acted out within that 'theatre', and becomes a play within a play within a play . . ."

Has he, therefore, found directing exciting, a challenge? "I sat there in New York playing with ideas and Jenny, the designer, sent me a small model of the set and I played with that with little soldier figures, but in the end that became frustrating because it wasn't the real thing at all. The time actually to start drew nearer and I came back to England when the other two shows had opened. When I met them all I was, quite frankly, terrified, but once I'd got my teeth into it I really enjoyed it.

"I found I tended to direct them on my feet. I had to be on

stage all the time – it was the actor in me, I suppose – but I just couldn't sit out there and watch them do it. I had to keep standing beside them, no doubt driving them mad, but walking with them so that I felt part of the play. The worst moment is when you have to divorce yourself from it and hand it over to the actors and say, 'Now it's yours, you take over.' That's the actor in me again."

Would he like to direct other plays after *Hamlet*? "Yes, I think I would. *Hamlet* has been special, though; it could never be like it again only because I know the play so well. I've directed it very much as an actor. I couldn't honestly say I've become a director because of this but it's given me some experience, not least of what it is like on the other side of the business, for instance, in the taking of decisions, answering people's queries, solving people's problems. The actor really only has himself to worry about: he's thinking, what are the problems in *my* character, in *my* role. Directing *Hamlet* you have twenty characters coming up to you and saying, 'I've got this problem, Derek . . .' and having to find answers for them as well. That's pretty tough.

"Then there are the technical decisions, sound, music, lighting, the wardrobe and not least the fights. There are all those decisions which actors are shielded from. I feel very grown up suddenly having to deal with them all.

"It's been enjoyable and fun. But whether it fits me to direct other things, I just couldn't say."

ALAN AYCKBOURN

Went into the theatre straight from school. Became a stage
manager with numerous touring and rep companies, joining
Stephen Joseph in his Theatre in the Round at the Stoke
"Vic" from 1962–4. Later followed Joseph to Scarborough
and took over as Director of Productions of Theatre in the
Round there in 1971. After working as an actor, in stage
management and as a director, he established himself as
one of the most successful playwrights the country has ever
produced. Continues writing plays, directs his own season
at Scarborough and, more recently, also began directing at
the National Theatre. Credits there include *'Tis Pity She's
A Whore* by John Ford. In 1989 will be joining Peter Hall
in the founding of a new company based on the Haymarket
in London.

On my way to see Alan Ayckbourn, I mistakenly got on
to a "football special", fortunately *en route* for the match.
The all-male travellers were intrigued as to why I was there
and, after explaining my mistake, I told them I was on my
way to see Alan Ayckbourn. "Cor," said one burly youth,
"he's brilliant! Did you see that play about the boat on the
telly?" Some had and some had not but one youth amazed
his friends by coyly admitting he had taken part in an amateur
production of an Ayckbourn play.

Ayckbourn's appeal spreads well beyond the regular
theatregoer but he is less well known as a theatre director,

although a recent clutch of productions at the National Theatre drew more attention to this. He has, however, directed plays in Scarborough for years, both his own and those of other writers, and has directed his own when they have transferred to London.

"I started out wanting to be an actor, directing came third or fourth. I never went to drama school. There was a master at school who was a real theatre nut and he used to take tours of schoolboy actors, first round this country and, later, abroad. I went on two of these 'Shakespeare' tours, one to Holland with *Romeo and Juliet* and then to the USA with *Macbeth*.

"It really clinched what I wanted to do. I'd been writing, mainly adaptations of the *Jennings* books (which might be described as illegal pirating) for school productions but they were really only vehicles to launch my acting career. So when I left school the French master, Edgar Matthews, used one of his contacts and got me a job with Donald Wolfit as an ASM and a walk-on part as a sentry. My one qualification for this was that I could stand for two hours without falling over and the last guy had fainted. So I actually saw working, at first hand, what must be described as the last of the great actor-managers, and I thought all actors were thus and was rather disappointed when I found out they were usually rather more mundane.

"So there I was, seventeen years old, at the Edinburgh Festival and working for Donald Wolfit, which was magic. Through another contact, Robert Flemyng, I got a job at Worthing Rep and worked there and then finally established myself at Leatherhead, still as an ASM but this time as an *acting* ASM.

"After that, the really major thing happened. I fell into Stephen Joseph's company. He was looking for a stage manager. I'd only ever worked in proscenium arches. Back in the late fifties, theatre in the round was virtually unheard of here. Joseph was the most extraordinary man. He generated tremendous excitement and he was a great visionary in the theatre. He was a man who not only did unconventional productions in the round in a seaside town which was known for things like the *Black and White Minstrel Show* and *An Evening with Val Doonican*, but he actually put on all new work, by dramatists who were often working within the company.

"I didn't want to be part of the dramatists' scene to start with, I just wanted to be an actor, but he encouraged me, possibly because he saw that my acting was not all that remarkable. I was a better stage manager than I was an actor and it's one of the great truths of the theatre that actors are ten a penny but good stage managers are very rare and valuable people. Anyway, eventually I started writing myself a series of vehicles which I hoped would launch my acting career. Those first plays, directed by other people, were designed for me to be seen. I was very lucky indeed that such early writing was immediately staged. I'm in the unique position, in working in that theatre, of never having a play turned down! I think I'd burst into tears if it happened.

"Stephen used to say, 'Well, providing you finish it on time and it looks reasonable, I'll do it.' So that's how I learned the job.

"Then about that time Stephen began to think that I wasn't serving the place very well as an actor and gently suggested that I might try my hand at directing a production. I did *Gaslight* by Patrick Hamilton, which is a marvellous play to start with because unless you do something absolutely devastating with it, it will work anyway. So it was a very good way to ease my way in as a director. It was inevitable from then, although it took a couple more years, that I would start to direct my own work.

"It wasn't until about 1963–4 that I directed my first 'own' play but, in fact, the bulk of my work has always been other people's plays and I combined the roles of writer, actor and director for quite a long time. Then, after a while, the acting limb began to wither because I think, as a director, your acting perspectives tend to get shot to hell: you don't any longer have the total subjectivity you need as an actor because you are always checking out how other people are performing.

"There were some fairly basic restrictions on performances at Scarborough anyway. For instance, the library, where the theatre was, used to shut smartly at 10 p.m. so we had to be finished by then. I must say, however, that although it was not an intentional path, it was a pretty good training to be a director and, indeed, to be a writer if you've worked in all those branches of the theatre. I lit shows, I did the sound for them, I stage-managed, so I knew enough to be able to talk to people with some understanding of what their problems were.

"It also gave me experience of working on a very low budget. I asked Stephen, when he said I could do *Gaslight*, how much money I could have for it and he replied, 'Nothing'. I said, 'Thank you very much, it's a costume play,' and he said, 'Well, if you're pushed, then £5.' I've never thought infinite budgets helped anything very much. I mean, it was nice to spend lots of money on *'Tis Pity She's a Whore* at the National (1988) but I wouldn't want to do that all the time. It also makes you feel more guilty. If you spend a couple of hundred quid and it doesn't work, then you can live with that. It was quite a shock, really. I'm just going back to Scarborough and have just planned that season and to come back to the reality of having two or three thousand pounds as a production budget, after spending thirty times that on one show, is salutary. I don't want in any way to denigrate the National, but I honestly don't think what I do there is worth thirty times what I do in Scarborough. The expenditure between the large and small theatres is disproportionate but if you have a large theatre with a large stage, like the Olivier, then you have to fill both."

What attracted him, so well-known for his own comedies, to a stark Jacobean piece whose main theme is incest? "I'd finished the production I had been contracted to do at the National when Peter [Peter Hall] asked me to do another play in the Olivier. He suggested *The Alchemist* by Ben Jonson. I went away and read it and I couldn't understand a word; it is a terribly dense text. But I thought, well, I might be able to understand this if I work on it, but the prospect of getting the public to understand it rather daunted me. I know the Olivier Theatre is a brute, having done four or five shows there, and it works best when a play has a strong narrative – it has to have that narrative; you can't be doing with moody plays. In a place that size, you can't even see the moods!

"So I started diving in among the era of the narrative dramas and finally came up with John Ford's *'Tis Pity* . . . I read it right through and thought, this holds me from beginning to end. I'd never seen it done and when he killed her at the end I went, 'Oh!' because I was so ignorant about the whole play and how it ended. It made me enthusiastic to try to get this across to other people, so that is how the show was chosen.

"It made a nice contrast with what I had been doing there before. I'd started with the kind of plays I suppose people would expect me to do like *Tons of Money*. In fact, this was far and away the most difficult of them all for me to do. You see, you just can't afford to fail in farce, which is very frightening. With anything else people can say, 'That was quite interesting. It didn't all work but I liked how he did such-and-such,' but if something *doesn't* work in farce, then nothing works. I also realised fairly early on that *Tons of Money* had a nice central idea but it was full of the most extraordinary holes and we found ourselves thinking, 'But she *knows* he isn't her husband', or 'That isn't right', and in the end we decided that when it was first put on the audience must have been half-cut before they even arrived at the theatre and obviously didn't mind. But I wasn't at all sure that a modern Lyttelton audience would be that tolerant so we tried to close up the holes. I actually finished up re-working the text and I was glad I was also a writer! But it was very hard work – trying to be funny always is.

"Compared to that, Arthur Miller's *A View from the Bridge* was an absolute doddle. It's a wonderfully strong script and it was made easier still by having a wonderful cast.

"Everything just came together, and when that happens in a play it's marvellous. I actually do think that if you come to a point in rehearsal where the production is just not working and is too difficult, there should be a rule that you abandon it because if you really have got it wrong, from the start, it will never be any good. You can, of course, find yourself with technical problems like, say, over a difficult prop while the rest of the show is rolling along nicely: that's not what I mean. But if you've gone wrong way back, you can work your socks off but when the play opens it's never any good. That's a useful lesson for all directors to learn.

"Then I directed my own *A Small Family Business*. Normally I write and then go straight into directing, but it was different with this play. One of the reasons I broke from Scarborough for two years was to see if I could write without it, because I had never written in advance, as it were, and I found it very frightening. The deadline of 'we rehearse on Monday and the actors are waiting', is always a sufficient impetus for me to finish a play. So to cope with this new situation I told myself that I had now 'grown up' and could set my own deadline. In actual fact, I wrote the play and finished it a year ahead of when I had to direct it.

"This is necessary because the National has a huge turning circle; the cycle of plays is planned months ahead, like planning a military operation. You can't deliver a script to the National the day before they start rehearsing. Anyway, when I'd finished it I sent it straight off. It was the first script I'd submitted since the 1960s. Then there was a long silence, because it had to be seen by Peter, who was abroad at the time, and I'd also sent another copy to Michael Gambon who was doing *The Singing Detective* and was in no position to look at anything. This meant that I didn't hear from them for weeks and I began to wonder whatever was going on. Then, to my relief, Peter finally rang up and said it was fine. So I found myself, a year later, rehearsing the play with a group of actors and trying to remember whatever it was I had wanted to do with it at the time I wrote it. Also everything was on a much bigger scale than I was used to, because I generally run my own plays in at Scarborough first. But it was exciting because I was able to do things that are physically impossible at Scarborough, such as work on two levels. I'd always wanted to do what might be described as 'a doll's house play' and as an 'honesty' play was developing in my mind at the same time, I was able to weave the two together. Having said that, though, I did find the experience quite scaring."

So had he found directing the Ford play comparatively straightforward? "I wouldn't say that exactly. There are twenty-seven scenes in it and the first thing I realised was that it had to be kept cracking on. You have to keep the pace up otherwise you lose it as the plot is so complicated: there are so many threads weaving through it. You have to ensure you get that story line absolutely straight down the middle and then keep it moving. You could do it by using an absolutely bare stage. But I'd been working, in a limited way, with the Olivier revolve so I spoke to Roger Glossop [the designer] and said I thought it would be fun to unfurl it.

"I drew out a rough diagram of the scenes, and what happened next was quite extraordinary. I started to tell the story while, as I did so, moving around a cardboard model. I found that every time I came to the end of a section the Friar's cell appeared, and it became apparent that the play had a sort of rolling motion. I reached the point where I had decided to break it for the interval – at the end of Act III – and found it had gone round three times exactly.

"So I thought, this is tremendous, what an exciting idea, and I tried doing the same to the second half of the play, whereupon the whole thing fell apart. It did not work. Just before I decided to give up the whole notion, I tried again but this time moving the revolve anti-clockwise and, to my delight, it went round exactly three times again! The play unwound and worked perfectly. After that, I flung a few books of Escher drawings at Roger, saying I thought I wanted it to look illogical, and he came up with wonderful designs. That particular stage is a nightmare to work on – the actors get completely disorientated – but the final design had the effect I wanted, which was to tell the story as clearly as possible."

Although he had been directing his own work in London for ten years, people he feels, have been blinkered to him as a director, seeming to assume that his plays direct themselves. It was not until the series of plays at the National that he was finally taken seriously as a director and this is now leading to a greater diversity in his working life.

"Peter [Hall], who brought me to the National, is setting up a new theatre company, based on the Haymarket, which goes into production in 1989 and I'm invited to be a co-director. I shall provide his company with two shows a year. Simultaneously, Michael Codron has asked me to direct *Othello* with Michael Gambon. Michael baulked at the thought of playing Othello every night, so I suggested that I write a parallel play, obviously not anything like *Othello*, but using the same cast and set, and then we will run them alternately. So the play I've just finished does exactly that."

He likes working with actors he knows well – "most of us do, I think" – and has a special relationship with Michael Gambon. "I think my strength as a director is an ability to make companies. I can say now – because it's coming to an end – that I think our 'company' at the National has been a really jolly one. We were quite envied because we were the lot that sat in the corner laughing and the stage manager said we were an impossible bunch, but it was all good fun. I think it came from my years of doing the same thing in Scarborough."

His immediate programme is very full indeed, directing, writing and reviving plays as well as directing the whole Scarborough season. "I break my working life into blocks of writing and directing. Fortunately my writing hardly takes any time at all. I'm able to write while doing other things or, rather, think about what I am going to write. For instance, when I was working on *'Tis Pity* . . ., a new play was stewing away and it was a good thing to have something else to think about. The physical writing process only takes me about a week, as before that happens the whole play has been worked out inside my head, which is one of the reasons I keep directing. You can't hang around waiting for that one week, waiting for the right time when you can sit down and write a play.

"I do think that period of being inside one's own head for about eight weeks as a writer is wonderful, but then so is directing. They are both extraordinary crafts and they interact. I think directing the Ford play helped me, as a writer, really to appreciate narrative plays and I've become more and more excited by them.

"As to directing, I remember what Stephen Joseph once said to me. It was when I was wrestling with that first play, *Gaslight*, and I asked him what directing was about and he replied, 'You have to create an atmosphere in which the actors themselves can create.' I said, 'Thank you very much', but, of course, it's the most difficult thing to achieve. I've been trying to do so ever since."

WENDY TOYE

Has worked for sixty-seven years in the professional theatre, having produced a ballet at the Palladium when she was only ten. Best known initially as a dancer and choreographer, later directed a string of West End successes which takes up two columns of *Who's Who in the Theatre*. Also directed numerous films. Credits include revues such as *These Foolish Things*; musicals such as *Bless the Bride*, *Tough at the Top*, *And so to Bed*, *Show Boat*; *Die Fledermaus* by Johann Strauss, the splendid 1965 *Orpheus in the Underworld* by Offenbach. Most recently was called in to rescue the musical *Ziegfeld*.

Few, if any, working in the theatre today can have as wide-ranging experience as Wendy Toye – she has worked in dance, opera, musicals and straight drama.

"Recently I was asked to write an article about my early days in dance and I thought about it and my time with Ninette de Valois and what I was doing when I was so very young, and I thought, for the first time ever, I wonder if I should have left that world? When I left it (at about eighteen years of age), I had had a very bad appendicitis and had to have an operation. In those days the recovery wasn't so quick and it was ages before I was allowed to dance again. I'd been given lots of opportunity to choreograph when I was very young and had been encouraged by many people, including de Valois and Anton Dolin, and I had also accepted choreographic jobs in the straight theatre, shows like *Strike a New Note*, with the late Sid Field.

"It was in 1938 that I persuaded George Black to let me involve ballet dancers with the conventional chorus line. I'm sure this was the first time it had happened in England. There had been shows with ballets in them but I believe I was the first to mix the styles and I was able to do this because of my versatile training, being as good a tap dancer as I was a classical and jazz dancer."

In fact, she was kept so busy choreographing shows that she never returned full time to serious ballet although she remembers with pride that she danced in most of the ballets in both the de Valois and Rambert repertoires, as well as with the Markova-Dolin company.

"I don't think I had seriously thought about directing and it was the great C. B. Cochran who first asked me to. He wrote to me and sent me a script of a musical called *Big Ben* and I wrote back and said I didn't see any reason for any dancing in the show and wondered what it was exactly that he wanted me to do. He replied saying that was just what he had wanted me to say, because he didn't see any dancing in it either, but that he wanted me to direct it.

"He had followed my career quite closely. I'd won a first prize in the Charleston Ball as a child of nine, and the only child entered. I won the female prize, Lew Grade won the section for men! Among the judges were Fred Astaire, Ziegfeld and the Dolly Sisters and it was organised by C. B. Cochran. He always remembered me as Number Sixty-six, which was my number in that competition.

"After *Big Ben* I directed *The Shepherd Show*, presented by Firth Shepherd and starring Douglas Byng, Arthur Riscoe, 'Monsewer' Eddie Gray, Richard Hearne ('Mr Pastry') and Marie Burke – a very awesome group for a young person to cope with. Then came *Bless the Bride* at the Adelphi Theatre. It was designed by Tania Moseiwitsch and written – as were other Cochran shows – by A. P. Herbert and Vivian Ellis. Georges Guétary came over from Paris to appear with Lizbeth Webb in *Bless the Bride* and when he left the show after playing in it for two years, he and I formed a company of dancers called 'Ballet-Hoo' who performed four numbers with him in his *Tour de Chant* in Paris and all over France. The third Cochran show I directed was *Tough at the Top*.

"I think a mistake Cochran made – and he didn't make many – was that although he was still taking a lot of money with *Bless the Bride* and audiences and critics had liked Lizbeth Webb and Georges Guétary so much, he decided to take it off while it was still playing to capacity houses. He was afraid of losing the theatre because if the takings dropped below a certain amount, the theatre had the right to give the show a month's notice. He was so worried that, after three years, the takings of *Bless the Bride* would suddenly fall off, that he started rehearsing *Tough at the Top* with two new singers although it had been written for Webb and Guétary. The public just didn't take to *Tough at the Top*. It had an excellent cast, with George Tozzi and Maria d'Attili, and although perhaps not such a well-constructed piece as *Bless the Bride*, I think it was one of Vivian Ellis' most beautiful scores and if Liz and Georges had been in it I think it would have been successful.

"So, you see, that for someone starting a new career I was surrounded by the most remarkable people, all of whom were tremendously helpful. It was the same when I directed my first film, *The Stranger Left No Card*. That came completely out of the blue too. During the war I had helped an American, Captain George Brest, by directing and staging a show for the Eighth Army Air Force called *Soldiers in Skirts*. Then, in 1949, I was in New York doing *Peter Pan* with Boris Karloff as Captain Hook and Mr Darling, Jean Arthur as Peter Pan and with a score by Leonard Bernstein. It was then that George – who I discovered was the famous George K. Arthur of silent films – showed me a short story that he wanted to make as one of three short films. I gave him some ideas for it and suggested he should come to England and make it in Windsor."

A couple of years later he arrived in London and asked her advice on the project. She suggested the late Alan Badel to play the lead, Alix Stone to design it and Muir Matheson as musical director and, "I finally told him it was such a good story he should go right to the top directors, David Lean, Anthony Pellisier, etc. He came back to me a week later having got everyone I suggested, then he threw the script on to my lap saying, 'But you are going to direct it'." Stunned, she rang a number of eminent directors, including Lean, to ask what they thought, "and they all said, yes, have a go!"

Alexander Korda was so impressed with the film that he put both her and Alan Badel under contract. "Sadly, I only directed a few films for him before he died. I think if I could have gone on working for him he would have allowed me to do the highly fantastic sort of ideas that I had enjoyed, but my contract was somehow automatically turned over to Rank and I was given straight comedy to do.

"Among the many people in the film industry who showed faith in me was Ian Dalrymple – he really put his head on the block. So did Kenneth More. *Raising a Riot*, which I made with them, was a success and I owe a great deal to both of them."

Had she encountered any prejudice because she was a woman working in what was even more of a man's world in her early days? "No, I can't say I ever felt any prejudice against me as a woman. I was certainly not aware of any. I guess the fact that I was an established theatre director helped and it certainly didn't do any harm that my first film won the Cannes short film award. Of course, I don't know about the jobs I didn't get or wasn't asked to do. Some folk might say I wasn't considered for them because I was a woman, but I think it's much more likely that someone else was more suitable for them.

"In the late forties and fifties there were really only two women film directors, Muriel Box and me – but when they talk about women blazing a trail I'm very rarely mentioned. It's partly my fault because I never made a big deal of it on purpose, because I really believe in equality, proper equality, for everyone. I never wanted to get publicity for myself because of being a rare woman director, so I avoided it. I do think, though, that a woman really does have to be good at whatever she is doing, although the standard is now so high in the theatre that everybody has to know what they are up to."

She acknowledges debts to Stephen Arlen and Anton Dolin. "Stephen Arlen was Administrator for the Sadlers Wells Opera Company, with Norman Tucker as Artistic Director, and it was Stephen who first invited me to direct the company. It was his vision that saw Sadlers Wells Opera move to its larger home at the Coliseum and so become the English National Opera. It was a really sad moment for our profession when he died so young.

"Then Anton Dolin – he used to get rather bored in the middle of choreographing something and would hand it over to me to finish. This gave me invaluable experience and the fact that he had enough faith in me to let me take over from him gave me confidence. One of the jobs was a film called *Invitation to the Waltz* with a lot of dancers, in which I was playing a part as well as dancing. Dolin fell in love with Lillian Harvey, the star of the film, and was so busy during rehearsals, flying back and forth to Paris and Germany to be with her, that he handed the whole of the ballet over to me. It was fairly simple stuff and was merely a background to a scene between me, 'the Ballerina', and Lillian, supposedly one of the corps-de-ballet. But the studio never forgot that I had done the work and organised everything.

"So I really got my training on the 'factory floor', so to speak. There were no schools for training choreographers or directors in my young days. It was amazing to have had such chances."

Wendy has also directed straight plays. How different did she find the two kinds of theatre – musicals and straight plays? "If it is a small-cast play, it's very different from a large-scale musical. But then a small-cast musical is also very different from a large-scale straight play. A well-written play is scored as carefully as a beautifully orchestrated piece of music. One great difference is that a musical cast has to know its musical notes before one can start staging the numbers, whereas very few directors or actors want the lines to be learned before the cast starts working together on a straight play.

"There are exceptions, of course, and Noël Coward was one. I suppose this was because he was generally directing his own plays and knew exactly how he wanted each character portrayed, but generally the chemistry between one actor and another sparks off so much. They like to learn the lines along with developing the character. This is much more difficult to achieve in a musical as the cast have to learn the music and lyrics first, but if you attend all those rehearsals you can guide the interpretations. I like to have a very definite shape and plan for a production, so that if any one of the cast sees something quite differently and I like it, I still know what mood and shape we need in, say, ten pages' time.

"When you think of that superb production of *Nicholas Nickleby*, it was, in fact, a straight play but it had all the elements and complications of a full-scale musical, so it is difficult to compare. Every production has its own set of problems and that's half the interest for a director, I think, anticipating the problems.

"Opera's different again for you have to shape all the way through it and you are very controlled by the music. It says a lot of things to you, and a lot of things for you, and it has this enormously strong shape that you go by and if you are any sort of a musician, or are in sympathy with music and have talked it over thoroughly with your musical director and principal characters, then you should all be thinking along the same line. It is then very difficult to deviate from that line as the music controls you."

Her production of Offenbach's *Orpheus in the Underworld* for Sadlers Wells Opera (later the ENO) in 1965 became one of the best-loved opera productions of modern times, staying in the repertoire until very recently. Its boring, strait-laced Orpheus with his collection of stuffed birds, his awful mother, Calliope, the libidinous Jupiter and errant Eurydice, brought the house down, especially when the entire Olympic pantheon descended into the Underworld in a London Transport lift.

"When Norman Tucker and Stephen Arlen first asked me

to do it, I knew I didn't want it to be in any specific period. After talking it over with Malcolm Pride, the designer, he came up with a brilliant concept which was so witty that the whole production fell into place. Then we had a ball working on the details, like the Underground and Calliope suddenly realising that she had on the same frock (though in a different colour) when being presented to Juno, and the children being played by the long-suffering and very co-operative chorus on their knees, and placing the Bee Duet in a bathroom.

"When you have the sympathetic working relationship with your designer that I have been lucky enough to share on so many occasions, you really don't know, in the end, who has suggested what. When I had discussed it all with the late Geoffrey Dunn, who translated and re-wrote the libretto, I told him I didn't much like the character of 'Public Opinion' and could he think of some other angle for that part? It was he who came up with the idea of making her Calliope, Orpheus' mother. It worked a treat. It was one of the Sadlers Wells/ENO productions which lasted longest – twenty-one years. It was only finally replaced in 1987."

She found it upsetting that, in a recent biography of Sir Ralph Richardson, another director was credited with directing him in *A Midsummer Night's Dream* (1964), a production she still remembers with great affection. "I was thrilled to be asked to do it. David William was to direct *The Merchant of Venice*. When I went to see Sir Ralph it was like an audition for we had not met each other before. I went up to his lovely studio in Hampstead and Lady Richardson met me and we had afternoon tea and then she took me upstairs to meet him.

"He told me he wanted to do both productions fairly conventionally, but particularly *The Merchant*. He was prepared to be a little freer over *The Dream*. So I told him how I'd thought about it and that I was delighted that Carl Toms was going to design it and because of the way he saw it, and wanted to use the Mendelssohn music, then it had to be done in that way, fairly conventionally. But I did want it to be very lively. Then, quite suddenly, he opened a drawer and got out a photograph. It was a man in cricket clothes, with a long beard. 'Do you know who that is?' he asked and I said, 'Yes, W. G. Grace'. And I swear to you that's why I got the job. But what a remarkable thing to do.

"He was really very delightful and his mind was always shooting off at a million tangents. However, it clinched the deal. He was wonderful to work with but very much himself. I remember his having a very bad cold. It was during a rehearsal of *The Merchant* which I was sitting in on, as David Williams and I often came into each other's rehearsals, and they were doing a run-through with everyone in at least part of their costumes and making grand gestures and so on. There was Ralph, with his bad cold, in this very dark suit, a black overcoat, a rolled umbrella and a bowler hat. He went right through the whole play and instead of bowing to people he raised his hat! It was a most wonderful sight as if he were saying, 'This is how I'm dressed today, so this is how I'm going to play it'. He would not go near anyone or take his coat off because of his cold."

The Dream (in which Alan Howard and Julian Glover played Lysander and Demetrius, and Patsy Byrne and Barbara Jefford were Hermia and Helena) toured South America where Wendy went down with typhoid "and they had to leave me behind in Peru. But on every first night when we opened on that tour, Sir Ralph would come up to me and take my hand and squeeze it and then he'd walk away and in my palm there would be a tiny ornamental toad . . . I've got quite a collection of them. I adored him and am so grateful that I was able to work with him."

She is still working very hard indeed and has a soft spot for one of her most recent shows, a musical at the Watermill Theatre near Newbury, called *Once Upon a Mattress*, "where I worked with Sally Dexter. She was a student at LAMDA when I was directing *Babes in Arms* for them. She has enormous talent. It was a delightful show based on the story of the princess and the pea and we were all sad when it didn't transfer."

She has also directed a highly successful production of *Kiss Me Kate* for the Danish National Theatre in Aarhus and

Copenhagen. "It was played in Danish but all the cast could speak English, which made it much easier for me. It was designed by Patrick Robertson and Rosemary Vercoe. We used a revolve for it, so that we never had to use front cloths, and saw the 'show' as if we were watching it from the wings. The actors were quite splendid to work with, for it is the country's best theatre company. There were wonderful wardrobe facilities, a fine building and a huge budget.

"The leads were both excellent straight actors, with great voices, who had played many Shakespearean roles. They were terrific. The director of the theatre had waited five years to get these two actors there at the same time to play the leading parts. I had about five weeks to put it on, although some of the cast were performing in the evenings so I couldn't have them all the time.

"As I was choreographing it as well as directing it, I started with the dancers first on their own, then gradually I had the actors joining in with them. Not many of them could dance so I gave them all classes during which I taught them the steps which I then finally put into the show. So when we came to the big numbers, like 'Too Darned Hot', they all knew sequences of steps which we could put into the number. That way it's not so frightening for non-dancers.

"As I said before, with a play it's always better to leave some things to see how they develop in rehearsal, but you really can't do that with a musical as there are so many different strands. In that way, it's easier in a straight play because if you get an actor who says he just doesn't see something like that, then it doesn't matter, because you have a basic plan of the scene and can take in what he says. It has to be much tighter with a musical – although it's easier with a show like *Kiss Me Kate* which is tried and true and has been done many times, rather than with a new one.

"It's all very different nowadays, anyway. Actors are expected to be able to dance and sing as well as act – indeed, they want to. In that particular show the girl who plays Kate has to be a very, very good singer although it isn't necessary for her to be able to dance. But in most musicals now they have to be able to do it all – sing and act and dance and do all of them very well indeed." She attributes the success of the English musical in recent years in part "to choreographers becoming directors so that something can evolve in that way. It was *West Side Story* which made the real break-through, combining music with libretto and direction with choreography, and it took years to get together. Before that in, say, *Oklahoma* they sang and acted but then they had a different group of dancers pushing the story along."

She can now look back on sixty years of continuous work in the theatre, films and TV, an average of three productions a year since 1947. Does she have any regrets, apart from the nostalgic feeling that she should, perhaps, have stayed with dance?

"I often wonder what might have happened with my career if Cochran, Korda and George Black hadn't died when they did. They might have guided me into doing other things, Korda especially, because he knew what I could do. He saw a talent in me for working on slightly macabre and fantasy subjects and I think he would have encouraged me to pursue it. I feel I could have done better work in films if I had been given the opportunity to work on more imaginative subjects. Fifteen or twenty years ago fantasy was frowned upon, it was not liked. Now, of course, fantasy's in.

"The other area I wonder about is musicals. Just before George Black died he told me he was going to take over one of London's small theatres. At that time he, with Val Parnell, ran the London Palladium, of course, as well as the London Hippodrome and the Prince of Wales theatres and produced all the shows there. I had choreographed many productions for him. His idea, though, was to put on small musicals, written and composed by new people, as well as those already established, a sort of training ground for new talent combined with experienced folk. He was going to put me in charge of running it with him, finding and encouraging the talent. The shows would start small but, if they were successful and needed to be enlarged for a transfer, then that was to be allowed for. None of the productions was to last long and the project was entirely experimental. It was a great idea and very sad that he died before he could put it into action."

As she contemplates her current and future plans, she looks ahead to plenty of work: *Get the Message* for the Molecule Theatre of Science for Children, *Song Book* by Monty Norman and Julian More at the Watermill Theatre (which will be her fourth production there for Jill Fraser) and when she talked to me she had just been asked to take over and rescue *Ziegfeld* at the Palladium and put Topol into the leading role (her fifth collaboration with Harold Fielding). She had also worked on *The Great Waltz, Show Boat,* and as associate producer on *Singing in the Rain* at the Palladium, and *Barnum*.

Her career has certainly been exciting and varied and full of achievement.